Praise for
THE BEIJING LECTURES

"In this brilliant analysis of the coming to be of Strauss, Plato, and Nietzsche as philosophers and poets, Laurence Lampert reaches new heights and plumbs new depths. An extraordinarily rich and insightful book, thoughtful and beautiful in its execution. A masterful performance by a thinker and author at the height of his power."

—Michael Allen Gillespie, author of *Nietzsche's Final Teaching*

"*The Beijing Lectures* is a subtle and illuminating discussion of the three thinkers, of the connection between philosophical understanding and philosophers' political-theological activity, and of the art of writing that is central to this activity."

—Mark Blitz, author of *Heidegger's Being and Time and the Possibility of Political Philosophy*

"*The Beijing Lectures* presents a wonderfully vivid, illuminating, and thought-provoking account of three great philosophers, with special attention to their philosophic art of writing and to the philosophic lives they led. What makes this book especially thrilling is that it is a monument to a most significant intellectual event, what Lampert calls 'the best intellectual experience of my life': the encounter of a most distinguished scholar of philosophy with an audience of distinguished Beijing scholars and students, at a time of a momentous flowering within China of philosophic interest in philosophers both from the East and from the West, both classical and modern."

—Peter J. Ahrensdorf, author of *Homer and the Tradition of Political Philosophy*

"Laurence Lampert's *Beijing Lectures* sum up a lifetime of reading and thinking, of learning and discovering, and what a voyage it is. With laser focus, Lampert guides the reader through the artful writings of Strauss, Plato and Nietzsche. With grace, gratitude and joy, he leads us far beyond the received history of philosophy to uncover a scintillating tradition of philosophic poetry that illuminates both the past and the future."

—David Janssens, Tilburg University

"Laurence Lampert is among the very best guides to each of these magnificent thinkers, and no one has done more to develop the comparison among them. Regarding 'philosophic poetry,' Lampert argues powerfully that, between the lines, Plato's Socrates was appropriating a poetic ethos rather than attempting to vanquish philosophy's rival in the so-called 'ancient quarrel' between them. Deploying compact yet sparkling prose, the book does justice to both contestants along with Strauss, Plato, and Nietzsche."

—Peter Minowitz, author of *Straussophobia*
and "Getting 'Woke' with Socrates"

THE BEIJING LECTURES

Strauss, Plato, Nietzsche

THE BEIJING LECTURES

Strauss, Plato, Nietzsche

Philosophy and Its Poetry

LAURENCE LAMPERT

pdb

PAUL DRY BOOKS
Philadelphia 2024

In Memoriam
Laurence Lampert
20 April 2024

First Paul Dry Books Edition, 2024

Paul Dry Books, Inc
Philadelphia, Pennsylvania
www.pauldrybooks.com

Originally published in Chinese and English by
Huaxia Publishing House as part of their Hermes series

ISBN: 978-1-58988-190-7
Library of Congress Control Number: 2024935061

Printed in the United States of America

Contents

Foreword to the American Edition

I want to begin by thanking Professor Liu Xiaofeng for inviting me to give these lectures in China, in Renmin University. It is an honor to be invited and I am very grateful to Professor Liu. His invitation has given me the occasion to reflect on the work I have done for the past forty years and to summarize some of its main points.

My first reaction to the email inviting me to give lectures in China was my customary one ten years into my retirement: "No, thank you, I just want to read and write." But as I read on into the details of the email and thought about them for a moment, I realized, "No, this invitation I simply cannot turn down."

The invitation came from a Professor Peng Lei at Renmin University in Beijing, inviting me to give six lectures on topics of my own choosing, each two and a half hours in length. After completing the lectures in Beijing, I was to give three lectures at Zhejiang University in Hangzhou and then at Chongqing University in Chongqing. So of course I replied, "Yes, I would be honored to do them." And they turned out to be the most engaging and rewarding speaking assignments of my academic life. The chief reason for that was my audience at each of the locations: never have I had audiences as informed and responsive as these. The reason for the exceptional audiences has a name, Liu Xiaofeng.

Professor Liu Xiaofeng is much more than a professor. He is a supremely gifted thinker and a man of vision and action. His thinking and acting led him ultimately to found schools of Classical Studies at three major Chinese universities, where I was to lecture. These schools of Classical Studies offer doctoral programs in the classical traditions of both China and the West—"classics" being the works of the great ancient and modern thinkers in the traditions of East and West.

In the course of his own thinking, Professor Liu came to the view that China, officially atheist but with various forms of popular religion and superstition, could perhaps benefit socially from Christianity—and Christianity might also be valuable as the antidote to what he regarded as a rising nihilism in China. Consequently, he studied Christian theology and philosophy, receiving a PhD from Basel University with a dissertation on Max Scheler, the German philosopher and religious thinker. His study of Western political theology led him to Carl Schmidt and the books on Schmidt by Heinrich Meier. Through Meier, Professor Liu came to Leo Strauss and to my book *Leo Strauss and Nietzsche*. Professor Liu recognized in Strauss a contemporary thinker of singular importance because of his rediscovery of the philosophers' art of writing and, especially, because of his emphasis on the difference between ancients and moderns and on the contemporary relevance of ancient wisdom. Virtually singlehandedly, Professor Liu made Strauss a topic of discussion among Chinese intellectuals. And he saw to it that everything that was preserved of Strauss's writings be available in Chinese, even some things not yet available in English. Moreover, he set in motion a massive and ongoing project of translating into Chinese not only the classics but also the works of contemporary Straussians. And, also of great importance, he attracted numerous talented doctoral students who are now continuing and expanding his work at many universities throughout China.

Having learned something about Professor Liu and the schools of Classical Studies he established, I prepared even more assiduously than usual for my six lectures, writing them out word for word. In that months-long preparation I had the constant assistance of my former student and now colleague, George Dunn, who had years-long experience in China and knew my thinking about as well as I did myself. Together we settled on the topic, "Philosophy and Philosophic Poetry," the wording I had long used to express Western philosophy's two fundamental tasks at least since Socrates: to gain knowledge of the whole and to develop an edifying public teaching within which philosophy could be sheltered.

After arriving in Beijing, I consulted with Professor Peng Lei on how best to present my six lectures. We decided to print copies of each lecture and make them available some days before the lecture itself, aiming to forestall difficulties in listening to a long lecture in a foreign language. Expanding and rewriting each lecture kept me extremely busy while I was there. The lectures in this volume are the product of that process of honing my language to meet the needs of that audience.

I arranged my lectures to present the first two on Leo Strauss and the tradition of Western philosophy, then two on Plato and two on Nietzsche, allowing me to touch on some of the most important conclusions I had reached in my decades studying each of these thinkers.

I remember the seminar room vividly. In the middle was a very long, oblong polished wood table surrounded by chairs, with additional chairs against the side and back walls. All of the chairs were occupied, and additional chairs had to be added as the lectures proceeded. There came to be about forty auditors in all. We had decided to have a short break in the middle of the two and a half hours and an opportunity for questions at the end of each lecture.

The first question after the first lecture confirmed for me just how informed my audience was: the detail-filled question concerned Martin Heidegger's view of the history of Western philosophy in comparison with Strauss's and asked why I thought Strauss's should be preferred to Heidegger's. This was not only a good question but, quite by accident, one for which I was especially well prepared: my PhD dissertation had been on Heidegger's and Nietzsche's views of the history of Western philosophy, and while that was some forty-five years in my past, I knew very well the weaknesses and oddnesses of Heidegger's view. That question and answer led to other detailed questions and detailed answers that continued for well over an hour and a half. This was a simply exhilarating experience for me and a promise of what turned out to be the best intellectual experience of my life. Walking back from my first lecture to my hotel room in the light of the full moon, I was thrilled by this beginning to the two weeks I would spend with my fine Beijing audience.

On a long walk in the hills northwest of Beijing on a day between lectures, Professor Peng Lei first raised the possibility of publishing my lectures in Chinese. I welcomed that, of course, adding that a bilingual edition would be best. That book, meticulously prepared and beautifully produced by editors associated with Professor Liu, appeared in 2021.

Most of my earlier books had been translated into Chinese before my visit, but the translation of my most recent book, *How Philosophy Became Socratic*, actually appeared in the early days of my Beijing talks. I have the copy in which about thirty of the auditors signed their names, some adding brief comments—a very pleasant collegial feeling had developed among us, partly because of an evening spent in a relaxed social setting where we discussed the work of my auditors as well as mine. A highlight of my weeks in Beijing were my two hours-long Chinese dinners with Professor Liu and Professor Peng Lei and his wife, Dora, the editor of the bilingual Chinese edition of this book. We not only talked, but Professor Liu, seated next to me at the round table, helped me fish out particularly slippery pieces of meat and fish that resisted my attempts to snare them with my chopsticks.

My audiences for the three lectures I gave in Hangzhou and Chongqing were somewhat smaller, but they were similar in the most important respect: they, too, were well prepared and talented, and we had long discussions after each lecture. It was in Hangzhou, in particular, that associations and friendships were established that continue to this day, in part because two of the auditors there became translators of the books that I wrote in the years after these China lectures.

Finally, I find it deeply satisfying that my Beijing Lectures will now be available to an English-speaking audience, in their original English.

Preface

My titles describe my lectures. Two will be on Leo Strauss; two will be on Plato; and two will be on Friedrich Nietzsche. And all six will be about philosophy and its poetry. Another way of saying that is that my lectures will be about *esotericism* and *exotericism* as the art of writing practiced by philosophers. It is an art that allows the philosopher to convey what he *thinks*—the esoteric part—through what he *says*—the exoteric part—without saying directly or simply putting into words what he thinks. It is an art of writing that is both a showing and a hiding: the artfulness of the showing consists in the shown leading to the not-shown, to the hidden. And the hidden is always what matters most—what *you*, if you're interested but only if you're interested, can find out on your own. And finding it out, you will treasure it all the more because you found it out on your own. So the philosopher's art is a kind of temptation, a seduction of *you*, meant to win you to him and his thinking. The esoteric content that his art conveys to you, he offers as a gift to you, his special reader. And it ties you to him. And you're grateful. And you live a life of gratitude to him and what he's given you. You're *caught*. "All my writings are fishhooks," said Friedrich Nietzsche.

My first two lectures will be on Leo Strauss. Strauss rediscovered the philosophic art of writing and then wrote about it or disclosed it as no previous philosopher ever had. But even though Strauss made it a public topic, he too practiced it. He was true to the philosophic art that he rediscovered and he conveyed what he really thought only indirectly.

My second set of two lectures will be on Plato, the ancient Greek philosopher who stands as the model for philosophic writing in the whole of the Western philosophic tradition. But Plato's writings display *his* model, the philosopher Socrates who was his teacher and who never wrote anything, but who spoke and, in his speaking, practiced the art that Plato found a way of writing. Plato's writing put Socrates' speaking into a more permanent form that generated a whole philosophic tradition: Western philosophy. Since Plato, Western philosophy is exoteric and esoteric, or, it is political philosophy and philosophy. In words that make political philosophy more explicit, it is a theological-political program and it is philosophy. My titles call the theological-political program *philosophic poetry*, a term that goes back to Plato himself. And with respect to the history of Western philosophy as a whole, Nietzsche said that, since Plato, all theologians and philosophers have been on the same track.

Until him—until Nietzsche. And my third set of two lectures will be on Friedrich Nietzsche, the German philosopher who aimed to put philosophy on a different track. *Different*, but Nietzsche's track too distinguishes between esoteric and exoteric, philosophy and philosophic poetry, or, in the words that Nietzsche used, Truth and Art.

As for me, I am a scholar of philosophy, a reader, an interpreter of texts. In Nietzsche's good phrases, I am a *philosophic laborer* whereas he is a *genuine philosopher.* As a philosophic laborer, I judge Nietzsche to be the philosopher of our time, the philosopher to whom we have to pay the closest attention because he came to understand the whole sweep of Western philosophy since the early Greeks and therefore to understand *our time* with a clarity and depth exceeding anyone else's. For me, Nietzsche is the philosopher from whom we should *differ* only with the greatest caution.

LECTURE 1
Strauss Recovers the Tradition of Philosophic Poetry

I begin with Leo Strauss, the philosopher who rediscovered exotericism/esotericism and publicized it, choosing to make the distinction well-known after a century and half of Western philosophy during which it had been almost forgotten. In my two lectures on Strauss, I will deal first with his rediscovery of exotericism. And *exotericism* is the word I will consistently use in these lectures to name the whole practice of the philosophers. Others call it *esotericism*, but Strauss himself called it *exotericism* because it more literally describes what the writings are: *exoteric*. After discussing Strauss's rediscovery of exotericism, I will deal with something that is still disputed by some of Strauss's followers: that Strauss himself practiced exotericism. I will show *that* he did and *how* he did it, by looking at things he said about Plato and then about Nietzsche.

ONE
Strauss's rediscovery of exotericism: his letters to Klein

Strauss left a record of his rediscovery of exotericism in letters that he wrote to his best friend, Jacob Klein, in 1938–1939 when he was thirty-nine and forty years old.

These letters deserve to become famous. They were written in German and have been translated into Chinese so you can read them. But they have not yet been translated into English, so many of Strauss's English-speaking followers do not know them or know them well. Those who have not would be shocked to read them, because Strauss is completely open here. The letters differ from all his publications in that openness. They deserve to become famous because they are so open and so radical. There has even been a debate in American Strauss circles whether they should have been published by Heinrich Meier at all in his edition of Strauss's works.

They are of course, *private*; Strauss wrote them to his best friend, who also spent his life studying the philosophers. But Strauss must have known that they would become known, because he knew that his writings would make him famous and that those that he attracted would want to read everything he had written, including his letters. After all, Strauss himself paid close attention to Plato's letters, Machiavelli's letters, Nietzsche's letters. And he could very easily have destroyed them—he could have asked his best friend to burn them. He did not do that. We must read them.

The letters cover about forty-four pages in Meier's edition, and what I will do is read selections from them in chronological order from January, 1938, to October, 1939, and make comments on the selections I have chosen. I'll skip some letters entirely and I'll read only parts of the others. If you read everything in the letters of these nearly two years you get a good picture of Strauss in a time of real stress and worry about his family, his not having a job, the dangerous situation in Germany shortly before the Second World War—writing privately to his best friend, Strauss expresses his deep concerns. But even those concerns cannot detract from the primary mood and feeling in the letters—extreme excitement and joy at discovering what the philosophers had written as if it were just for him, which in way it *was*, and excitement at what he would have to report to a world that had become ignorant of what the philosophers really wrote and therefore ignorant of what philosophy is. The selections I have picked out concern only his rediscovery of exotericism.

The letters begin with Maimonides, whom Strauss had already studied for years as the most important philosopher in the Jewish tradition, and who lived in the twelfth century of Western time calculation (c. 1135–1204), more than seven hundred years before Strauss studied him. In his first book, *Spinoza's Critique of Religion*, which had already been published in 1928, Strauss said of Maimonides that he was "a believing Jew." Now, ten years later he said this:

> **The Letter of January 20, 1938**
>
> Maimonides "was a truly free mind . . . The crucial question for him was not world-creation or world-eternity (for he was persuaded of world-eternity), instead, it was whether the ideal lawgiver must be a prophet."

Maimonides was persuaded of the eternity of the world: that was the position of *philosophy*, not the position of the *Bible* and so not the position of a believing Jew. Strauss now saw that Maimonides rejected the Bible's view, the Jewish view, of the creation of the world. The question for him had become "must the ideal lawgiver be a prophet?" Judaism is a tradition of *law* and the Jewish lawgiver was Moses, the most important figure in the Jewish Bible. In Plato the *philosopher* is the ideal lawgiver. So the question as Strauss now saw it was this: Must the philosopher-lawgiver also be sent from God? That is, be seen as sent from God, present himself as sent from God?

> It's very difficult to prove that because he discusses the question in an exegetical form.

For those who read Strauss today, this is *funny*: the exegetical form is the form of a commentator, and a commentator can hide his own view of what he's commenting on; he can appear to be merely reporting. Maimonides did that and made it hard to prove what he himself thought. And *Strauss* did that—he chose to write as a commentator. So it is very difficult to prove what Strauss thinks because he, like Maimonides, chose an exegetical form of writing.

> **February 16**
>
> You can't imagine with what infinite refinement and irony Maimonides handles "religion." . . . If in a few years I explode this bomb (in case I live so long), a great battle will be kindled.

It is completely clear to Strauss what the implications are of revealing what he is discovering in Maimonides: he holds a *bomb* in his hand, a bomb that will explode the whole tradition of understanding Maimonides. The explosion will be deeply destructive because Maimonides is the greatest teacher of Judaism, its most respected and authoritative teacher.

> This will yield the interesting result that a simply historical determination—the determination that Maimonides in his beliefs was *absolutely* no Jew—is of considerable present-day significance: the incompatibility in principle of philosophy and Judaism would be demonstrated to the eye.

The "historical determination" is what a reader of the writings can learn, a historian like Strauss, reading them as an exoteric writing hiding an esoteric meaning for *you*, Maimonides' special audience, whom he educates in the forbidden things because *you*, his special reader, are like him. So Strauss says that the science of history that is aware of the art of writing can show that Maimonides was *absolutely no Jew*. To be a philosopher, to depend wholly on *reason*, absolutely rules out being a Jew, which depends on *faith*, on what is written in the sacred book that the Jewish tradition holds is a *revelation* directly from God. Being a Jew depends on *obedience* to the laws given in that Revelation. Strauss maintained this major point throughout his life: the radical incompatibility of Revelation and Philosophy. Revelation establishes a tradition of *obedience*. Philosophy attempts to gain a *free mind* that can accept as true only what reason can demonstrate.

> An essential point in Maim.'s technique is *of course* that he says *everything* completely openly, if in the places where an idiot doesn't look.

You have to be careful here: An *idiot* is almost every reader. It's me; it's you. And *completely openly* means open only to the one whose skeptical free mind knows how to look for what almost every other reader does not look for. This is a most important point: the esoteric is not hidden somewhere beneath the surface or above the surface: it's *on* the surface but still hidden, hidden in plain view, if you know how to look. One of Strauss's best sentences says this: "The problem inherent in the surface of things, and only in the surface of things, is the heart of things."

> There's an aphorism in N.: when I hold the truth in my fist, dare I open my fist?

"N" is Nietzsche. N. is enough. Both Strauss and Klein know that N. can only be Nietzsche. (I've been informed that the Chinese translator did not know the N. was Nietzsche; he wrote simply "somebody.") In 1935, three years earlier, Strauss had said in a letter that "Nietzsche so dominated and charmed" him between his "22nd and 30th year" (1921–1929) "that I literally believed everything I understood of him" (letter to Löwith June 23, 1935). I haven't been able to find those exact words about holding "truth in my fist" in N. But the thought is certainly his. He spoke of three basic matters that were "true but deadly": "the sovereignty of becoming, the fluidity of all concepts, types and kinds; and the lack of any cardinal difference between man and the animals." And Nietzsche constantly faced the question that the philosopher faces—"dare I open my fist" on the deadly truths? I'll talk about that in my Nietzsche lectures, but it is important to recognize from the start that the "deadly truth" is not deadly to *him*; he lives easily with it; he celebrates it because he seeks the truth and loves the truth. But he knows that it is deadly to society, deadly to the beliefs on which society depends for its health.

> July 23
>
> I could actually be a bit proud that I've solved this riddle. But maybe my nerves aren't strong enough—or I lack "*scientia*"—or both are the case. In short, at times I shudder in the face of what I may cause by my interpretation. The upshot will be that I, poor devil, have to spoon up the soup in which this diabolical sorcerer of the twelfth century landed me.

I quote this personal remark by Strauss partly because it shows that he has a clear sense of where he stands: he knows how monumental his discoveries in Maimonides are. But I quote it mostly because it says something I don't hear in any of his publications: *doubt* about whether he can do it. Are his nerves strong enough? Can he bear the strain of this radical, even destructive unorthodoxy? Does he lack the knowledge or the nerve? Here he asks himself if he is strong enough in his *intellect* and his *will* to bear the burden of really learning what the philosophers know and of making it known to others.

Up to this point in the letters, Strauss's radical discoveries are confined to Maimonides. In his 1935 book, *Philosophy and Law*, Strauss had dealt with Maimonides and his *predecessors*; but there his predecessors were the Islamic philosophers, philosophers also raised in a tradition based on Revelation, on a book to which the believer had to submit, to surrender his intellect. But the Islamic philosophers pointed to *their* predecessors, the Greeks, to *pagans*, thinkers raised outside the tradition of obedience to Revelation.

It is at this point in his letters that Strauss turns back to those Greeks. That means that his letters to Klein do not discuss the exotericism of the Islamic philosophers who influenced Maimonides.

> October 15
>
> I'm now reading Herodotus, who—I swear it as a Catholic Christian—is also an esoteric writer and one in perfection. In short, it's happening again.

"Catholic Christian" is a nice little joke by Strauss. So the first Greek Strauss turns to is the "historian" Herodotus, and not a so-called philosopher. (As a student at a classical *Gymnasium* in Germany, Strauss learned Greek and Latin, and read the classics. And he kept reading them. But just why he turned to Herodotus as the first Greek after his discoveries in Maimonides he does not say.)

> **October 20**
>
> I'm really stunned, and prostrate myself before such artistry (= capability). My lucky star wants it that his work is really the single model for Plato known to me.

Strauss bows down on the ground as before some god, honoring Herodotus for his mastery as an esoteric writer. But it's not Herodotus who is of the highest interest to him, it's *Plato*—and when he reads Herodotus he thinks of Plato as following the model not just of Socrates but of the writer Herodotus.

> I can therefore show that what is nearest my heart about Plato is independent of the specifically Platonic philosophy.

This is a genuine *bomb.* He splits Plato in two: "the specifically Platonic philosophy" would be what we can call the *exoteric* Plato, the *teaching* Plato taught. And *that* is separate from what is nearest Strauss's heart—the esoteric Plato about which Strauss would have heard nothing from the scholars of Plato who had for a century abandoned the idea of an esoteric Plato. Strauss can *show* that distinction—he can interpret Plato's text as he can interpret Herodotus's text. The bomb is that Strauss can show that Plato himself did not *hold* what he *teaches.* And it's that hidden Plato that Strauss loves. And with that we're at *the basic matter.* Plato is the teacher of Maimonides and Maimonides' Islamic predecessors—and he was a teacher of the necessity of exotericism even though he was not raised in a tradition of Revelation as were Maimonides and his Islamic predecessors.

> **November 2**
>
> I find myself in a state of frenzy that's consuming me: after Herodotus now Thucydides too!

I include this state of frenzy because of the next letter:

> **November 27**
>
> Herodotus, Thucyd, and Xenophon are *no* historians—of course not—but authors of exoteric . . . writings.

All three great ancient Greek historians wrote exoterically. This is the *first reference to Xenophon* in Strauss's letters on discovering exotericism. Xenophon's *The Education of Cyrus* is

> a wholly great book of sublime irony, what Socrates is is shown through his caricature of Cyrus. Only through that medium does Xenophon show the true, hidden Socrates whereas he shows the manifest Socrates in his *Memorabilia*. His Socrates-image is therefore *not fundamentally* different from that of Plato.

Strauss moves very rapidly. Just a few weeks after discovering *Thucydides'* exotericism, he can already say what *Xenophon's* writing strategy is: *Xenophon* shows the truth about the most important of all persons for him, Socrates, through a caricature of a *king or ruler*, a figure most people will think is more important than a mere philosopher. Cyrus is the founder of the Persian Empire, a *ruler* who *founds a whole empire*, a ruler who is a *practical* and not a *theoretical* man. What Strauss sees is radical: the true, hidden Socrates is, in his very different way, a kind of *ruler* and a kind of *founder*. Through Socrates, a theoretical man, a *philosopher*, a new kind of empire comes into existence, the empire of a philosophic ruler. And Xenophon, a student of Socrates, shows that in his artful writing.

In the Western classical tradition Plato has almost always been held to be more important than Xenophon as a guide to Socrates. But traditionally Xenophon was given a very high place right next to Plato. In Strauss's time, however, more than a century of modern scholarship had completely destroyed Xenophon's reputation as great. And the reason was that the classical scholars had completely abandoned the tradition of exoteric reading. One of Strauss's greatest achievements is his recovery of Xenophon, the genuine Xenophon, the philosopher. Strauss's first published essay on the ancient Greeks was on Xenophon; it was published in 1939 while he was making these discoveries in exotericism. And Strauss's first book on the Greeks, *On Tyranny*, was on Xenophon's *Hiero*. And the two books that Strauss said were his best books were his two late commentaries on Xenophon.

There is another crucial point in the letter I just cited: Xenophon's Socrates is "*not fundamentally*" different from Plato's. That is completely against the view of all the scholars when Strauss wrote it. And it is a major insight: Socrates, the fundamental teacher, can be understood through Plato and through Xenophon. Both allow the esoteric Socrates to be seen, one can help illuminate the other because the two Socrateses are not fundamentally different.

> **December 2**
>
> I'm curious about what is hidden in Sophocles who, according to tradition, was a friend of Herodotus—I'm afraid that here too it's philosophy and *not* the *city and the ancestors.*

I include this remark in order to show the *scope* of Strauss's recovery of the Greek writers: *Sophocles* is one of the three great writers of tragedies in classical Athens. Strauss himself never published anything that demonstrated his suspicion here, but his most outstanding follower, Seth Benardete, did.

> **February 16, 1939**
>
> Xenophon is my special favorite because he had the courage to clothe himself as an idiot and go through the millennia that way—he's the greatest trickster I know. I believe that he does in his writings exactly what Socrates did in his life. In any case with [Xenophon] too morality is purely exoteric, and just about every second word has a double meaning.

Xenophon dared to clothe himself as an idiot—and the whole of modern scholarship believed he *was* an idiot. A "trickster" is a swindler, a cool confident person who wins your trust in order to cheat you, to steal from you.

And if Xenophon does what Socrates did *Socrates is a trickster, a swindler.* This is very serious—it's the ultimate bomb about Socrates. Socrates is taken to be—and is—the greatest philosophic teacher of morality; he is the heroic model of the teacher of morality, but the morality he teaches is wholly exoteric. Strauss proves that he is right about this bomb:

> *Kalokagathia* was, in the Socratic circle, a swear-word, something like "*philistine*" or "*bourgeois*" in the 19th century.

Kalokagathia is two Greek words taken together in order to describe the Greek gentleman, the pillar of civic life in the Greek civil order. The two words are *noble* and *good.* And what did that word for the *gentleman*, the noble and good man, mean inside the Socratic circle? It was a word of *ridicule* used to diminish and mock. But we cannot forget that Socrates is the teacher of virtue to the young Greek gentlemen with whom he conversed. Socrates is the teacher who gives these young gentlemen good reasons for continuing to follow the virtue of their fathers and forefathers. What Strauss says is that that teaching is *exoteric*, and the exoteric masks a genuine understanding that sees the true grounds and limits of the gentleman's virtue. Both matters are important: Socrates' exoteric moral teaching is a teaching of virtue for the young gentlemen; his true understanding of the virtues is to be learned by the very few like himself. Socrates' speech about morality has two meanings, one for each of his two audiences.

> And *sôphrosunê* is essentially self-control in the expression of opinions.

Sôphrosunê is the Greek word for *moderation* or *self-control*, one of the four classical virtues with courage, justice, and wisdom. What does Strauss discover *self-control* to really mean within the Socratic circle? Self-control in speaking; *moderation* means *exotericism*; it means *controlling and guarding* what you say or write. So the philosopher reinterprets the virtues of the gentleman to have a different sense for *him* and his kind. *Philosophic* moderation means in part continued use of *the old moral words* but understanding them in a radically different way. The philosopher's moderate, moral *speech* shelters his radical *thinking*.

> —in short, there's a whole system of secret words here exactly as in Maimonides, therefore a found feast for me.

You have to be careful with "*secret words*"—they are the common words like the words for the virtues. They are *secret* only in meaning something unspoken and different for the thinker.

> **July 25**
>
> The identity of Xenophon's and Plato's Socrates is beyond doubt, it's the same Socrates-Odysseus in both, the *teaching* too. The problem of the *Memorabilia* is identical to that of the *Republic*: the problematic relation between justice and truth, or between the practical and theoretical life.

Xenophon's *Memorabilia* and Plato's *Republic* treat the same issue: the problematic or questionable relation between the *practical* and the *theoretical* life. Only in his published writings does Strauss spell out that "*problematic relation*." The practical life is based on *loyalty* to common values or moral virtues that society holds to be true; the theoretical life is based on a *passion to know*, and it comes to know that the virtues to which all are loyal are in the fundamental sense not true but only necessary. There is no need for Strauss to explain to Klein what the problem in the problematic relation is, because Klein already knows. Put briefly that problem is this: what the *philosopher*, the one who lives the theoretical life, comes to know can destroy the foundation of the society of which he is a part. And if the *society* comes to learn what the philosopher thinks, it can destroy him—it will see him as an enemy and could do to him what the Athenians did to Socrates, kill him. The problematic relation of the practical and the theoretical life leads the philosopher to exotericism. Exotericism protects society from philosophy and protects the philosopher from society. There are other reasons for exotericism besides this problematic relation, and I have already touched on the main one: it is a temptation, a seduction to the philosopher's young kin.

Notice that in this letter Strauss calls Socrates, "*Socrates-Odysseus.*" Odysseus is the wisest man in Homer and in his poem, *The Odyssey*, wise Odysseus becomes a *philosopher.* But Strauss's main point here depends on Odysseus's reputation for being *wily*, being a trickster, a liar who cannot be fooled. I mention that because Odysseus will appear in my first Plato lecture as the model for Socrates.

> **October 10**
>
> [Hesiod's *Theogeny* is] an answer to the question of what the first, the unborn things are; further, an illumination of the Olympian through this question; and finally, an enlightenment of what this question and answer mean, that is, what wisdom means. The first things are not the gods but such things as earth, sky, stars, ocean which at one place are expressly distinguished from the gods simply.

I include this mostly because it extends the great fact of exotericism back to the founding Greek poets, Hesiod and Homer. Their poetry is exoteric. Hesiod's *Theogeny* is his poem of the birth of the gods; it is authoritative for everyone, but the way it is written allows a few to learn "*What the unborn things are*"—the things that always are, the natural things, the things more important than the gods to one who seeks understanding. Learning what the unborn things are illuminates what *the Olympians* are; it shows what the gods who care about the human things are: the inventions of wise poets like Hesiod. And this enlightenment shows what wisdom is: wisdom is knowledge of nature and human nature, and knowledge of what a god is. What Strauss is discovering in these letters are the very matters that will occupy him for his whole life.

> I'm convinced it's not different in Homer.

Strauss moves from Hesiod to Homer, the most important of poets, the one Plato calls "the educator of Greece." Strauss believes that "*it's not different in Homer*" than in Hesiod, but he does not develop this insight either in his letter or in publications. But Seth Benardete did: *The Bow and the Lyre* on Homer's *Odyssey* demonstrates that the founding *poet* of Greece is also its founding *philosopher.*

> **October 25**
>
> I've now understood [Plato's] *Symposium* in principle: it's the "authentic" enlightenment about the profaning of the mysteries by Alcibiades; not Alcibiades but Socrates blabbed the secret of the mysteries. It's a case of the famous fact that the actual "accuser" of Socrates is Plato.

This is the last of Strauss's letters to Klein that I will mention. I include it because it singles out Plato's *Symposium*. In a lecture course at the University of Chicago from 1959, twenty years later, Strauss showed why he regarded the *Symposium* as the most important of Plato's dialogues because it reveals the real secret of the mysteries. I will talk about this in my second Plato lecture because what happens in the *Symposium* is of the greatest importance. For now, I want to mention only one thing from the letter. Socrates "*blabbed*" the secret of the mysteries—to *blab* means to *say too much*, to *say what you shouldn't say*. The "*mysteries*" were the core of Athenian religion, and Athenians were initiated into that religion through special secret rituals and rites. Once initiated, the initiates were strictly forbidden to say what the rites were—they were the *mysteries* and they were to be kept secret. But the mysteries Socrates *blabbed* in the *Symposium* are the secret truths about *philosophy* and the *philosopher.* Those truths will be the most important things I will have to say about Socrates becoming Socrates in my second Plato lecture.

And with that I end my report on Strauss's letters to Klein, the letters in which he reported his recovery of philosophic exotericism on the very days he was making his discoveries. Strauss's letters to Klein are unlike anything Strauss ever published, because in the letters he opens his fist on the bomb, first about Maimonides but then about Socrates and Plato and Xenophon. The letters to Klein give the readers of Strauss's other writings direct access to what he learned about exoteric writing in the very months in which he was learning it. And they give direct access to what Strauss thought. The letters help settle any argument about Strauss's real views.

But after Strauss made the discoveries recorded in these letters, how *did* he explode all those bombs he held in his hand about the philosophic tradition? He very soon developed a strategy for presenting his discoveries in a way that made sure that they did not explode immediately and obviously. His strategy was itself indirect. We could say that he provided his bombs with a long *wick*, a long string that he lit in you, the reader, a string that would burn in you and lead you slowly, through your own discovery of what he is really saying; the bomb would explode for *you* and only after long work. Strauss's strategy taught you to read at the same time that it was teaching you what was really there in a philosophic author.

So Strauss developed his own manner of exoteric writing which was much more open than the traditional manners and which would eventually establish a tradition of reading that would make the philosophers' *esoteric* understanding more generally available. And he spent much of the rest of his working life writing about the great philosophers of the tradition—and doing it successfully, as the global spread of his writings and the global character of his readership demonstrates.

But the 1938–39 letters to Klein give clear access to what is of enduring importance in Leo Strauss: studying the letters can anchor the way we read Strauss and help us in reading the philosophers generally, reading them with constant attention to the two-fold character of their writings: what they teach on the surface and what they lead or tempt a reader to infer from the surface.

For the rest of my lectures on Strauss I'm going to talk only about his studies in the history of philosophy, and only about his studies of Plato and Nietzsche. That means I am going to *ignore* the other great topics to which Strauss devoted himself, including his very important work analyzing present-day philosophy with a view to understanding why it had lost or forgotten the exoteric tradition, a loss that threatened to become permanent because current philosophic trends argued powerfully for the impossibility of philosophy, the impossibility of understanding the truth of things.

For Strauss on Plato and Nietzsche I will discuss two texts only, one on Plato and one on Nietzsche. Both deal with *philosophy* in a way that is intended to show that *philosophy* generates or gives birth to *philosophic poetry*. Both the Plato text and the Nietzsche text are short, but they are taken out of longer texts and their meaning in part depends on their setting within those longer texts. I will look closely at the words of the short texts and occasionally appeal to the setting in the larger texts. What I have to say will make clear that Strauss gave us, *his* readers, the same difficulty Maimonides gave his reader: like Maimonides, Strauss discusses philosophy and philosophic poetry in an exegetical form which makes his own view available only to inference.

The point of my discussing these texts is partly to show that Strauss wrote exoterically, but more importantly to show that Strauss made it possible for us to see the exoteric character of Plato's and Nietzsche's writing. I begin with Plato, with Strauss's most important statement on Plato: the central essay of *The City and Man*, "On Plato's Republic." I discussed this essay in detail in *The Enduring Importance of Leo Strauss*.

TWO
Strauss's essay on Plato's *Republic* in *The City and Man*

Strauss's essay "On Plato's Republic" has two parts separated by a little mark of punctuation: a dash at the end of paragraph 13. The first thirteen paragraphs are on how to read a Platonic dialogue. Then comes the dash. Then the rest of the essay, an interpretation of the *Republic*, sixty-five paragraphs that can be considered as one separate, complete unit. The central paragraph of the sixty-five paragraphs is the thirty-third, and it deals with the central matter. That paragraph has thirty-eight sentences. Its center, the nineteenth and twentieth sentences, are two questions. I will focus on those two questions.

I have to say two things about what I'm doing here.

First: Strauss taught that all that the greatest writers *hid* the central matter in the central place. He called that "*the least exposed place*" compared to the most exposed beginning and end. But Strauss's emphasis on centers made the center the most exposed place. Did Strauss himself follow the greatest writers in this technique of writing? Of course he did. All his writings show this art of centering.

Second: You can't just look at centers. To understand the center you have to earn it, you have to work to see what prepares the center and what follows from the center. And you have to think about what all that means. What I'm going to say now is a kind of *cheating* or a kind of *crime*. It's never enough just to look at the center, but that's what I'm going to do.

Strauss's central paragraph begins on education in Plato's *Republic*, children's education through stories and songs. It is education through poetry, a most important word. Those stories and songs are typically about gods and heroes, figures whose actions are to be admired and mimicked by children. Plato's emphasis is on the right kind of stories that teach the right kind of behavior and warn against the wrong kinds of behavior. "To indicate the right kind," Strauss says, "Socrates lays down two laws" for the gods. Socrates presents a theology that in part consists of untrue stories about the gods.

Notice: Strauss quietly says that Socrates is a *legislator*, a person who lays down laws, and Socrates lays down laws for the gods. And, very importantly, new laws for the gods. The untrue stories are for little children, but Strauss says they are also "for the grown-up citizens of the good city." The untrue stories that the citizens absorbed as children are what the grown-up citizens believe: what is taken in during one's childhood is what one continues to believe and act on as an adult.

Socrates controls the conversation in the *Republic* and, as Strauss says, Socrates makes the conversation *shift* almost unnoticeably "from the demand for noble lies about the gods to the demand for the truth about the gods."

And now I'm at the part of the central paragraph that I want to read. I'll read Strauss's sentences and make comments on them.

> The speakers start from the implicit premise that there are gods, or that there is a god and that they know what a god is. The difficulty can be illustrated by an example.

It's not clear from the grammar of the sentence what the difficulty refers to, but it becomes clear: the difficulty is *knowing what a god is.*

> Socrates asks Adeimantus whether the god would lie or say the untruth because of his ignorance of ancient things and Adeimantus replies that this would be ridiculous (382d6–8). But why is it ridiculous in Adeimantus' view? Because the gods must know best their own affairs, as Timaeus suggests (*Timaeus* 40d3–41a5)?

These two questions stand at the center of Strauss's central paragraph. What Strauss placed at the center of his central paragraph on Plato's *Republic* is two questions about whether the god would lie because of his ignorance of ancient things.

First question: The first question is about *Adeimantus's* view of the gods. Adeimantus is one of the two young men who talk most with Socrates that night. He is a young man, noble and good in the way of a young gentleman, and his view of the gods would be the view he absorbed as an Athenian boy, the view passed down in the stories of Homer and Hesiod.

Now I have to pause here to say a little more about Adeimantus because it matters for what is happening here at the center. We know Adeimantus best from the long speech he had made earlier, a speech that helped force Socrates to take up the main question of the book: a defense of justice that was meant to persuade Adeimantus and the other young men that justice is better than injustice, being decent or moral is better than being immoral. In his long speech Adeimantus had expressed the beginnings of a moral rejection of the stories about the gods that he had been raised with, Homer's and Hesiod's stories about the gods. Adeimantus is a young man who has begun to lose his confidence in the stories about the gods that he had absorbed as a child.

To simplify and put that in a language familiar to us, young Adeimantus was beginning to experience a death of the gods. The Homeric gods, the old gods, the only gods he knew, were dying for him, and he had good reason to be deeply shaken by that: if the gods were *immoral* as the stories seemed to imply, if the gods could be *bought*, if the gods even supported the *wicked*, then there seemed to be no good reason to be just—and Adeimantus, decent and noble young gentleman, dearly wants to continue being decent and noble, to continue being just, but if the gods themselves are *unjust* why should *he* take that hard and difficult way himself? This is a most important point because it helps define the times in which Plato acts. Plato is careful to define those times through the speeches of Adeimantus and his brother Glaucon: it is a time of the death of the gods for decent young men who have been brought into touch with the Greek enlightenment.

Second question: The other question at the center is about Timaeus's view of the gods. Timaeus is a philosopher, though Strauss does not mention that here. He is the philosopher

Socrates will listen to in Plato's dialogue *Timaeus* as he lays out a whole cosmology, an account of the world as a whole. As a philosopher who shares the central place in Strauss's central paragraph with Adeimantus, Timaeus brings out what Adeimantus is not: Adeimantus is not a philosopher nor is he a potential philosopher. His interests lie elsewhere, with the poetry he learned as a boy and still loves and with the justice and decency that befits a young gentleman.

> It is true that Timaeus makes a distinction between the visible gods who revolve manifestly and those gods who manifest themselves so far as they choose, between the cosmic gods and the Olympian gods, and that no such distinction is made in the theology of the *Republic* where only the Olympian gods are identified.

The philosopher Timaeus makes a distinction with respect to the gods; he divides them into two categories of *cosmic* and *Olympian*, gods that are natural forces or entities like the sun and moon, and gods that are persons and who reveal themselves to humans. Strauss points this out because he wants to make the following point:

> But precisely this fact shows the "mythical" character of the theology or the gravity of the failure to raise and answer the question "what is a god?" or "who are the gods?"

So there is a *grave failure* in the discussion about the gods in the *Republic*, the failure to raise and answer the question "What is a god?" To understand that grave failure, I want to read something else. If you have studied Strauss's *The City and Man* you know how it ends. It ends with sentences I want to read now. So I interrupt our passage briefly to look to the end of Strauss's essay:

> . . . the pre-philosophic . . . city sees itself as subject and subservient to the divine in the ordinary understanding of the divine or looks up to it. Only by beginning at this point will we be open to the full impact of the all-important question which is coeval with philosophy although the philosophers do not frequently pronounce it—the question *quid sit deus*.

Notice that here at the very end of his book Strauss himself does not actually *pronounce* the question that the philosophers do not frequently pronounce: *What is a god? Or What might a god be?* Instead of pronouncing the question, he puts it in Latin. But in the central paragraph of his essay on Plato's *Republic* Strauss does pronounce it. He speaks of "the gravity of the failure" of Socrates and Adeimantus to "raise and answer the question 'what is a god?' or 'who are the gods?'" Whose fault is that? Is it Adeimantus's? Adeimantus shows himself in the *Republic* not to be a philosopher or a potential philosopher. Why did Adeimantus not raise the question? Because Adeimantus *has no question*. Adeimantus *knows* what a god is. A god is what Homer and Hesiod said a god is. Adeimantus's question is not *what is a god?* His question is why the gods aren't more just than they are, more moral than they are, more worthy of being trusted than they are.

Not raising the question is Socrates' fault. Like the philosopher Timaeus, the philosopher Socrates will have raised and answered the question of what a god is. But having raised and answered that question, the philosopher knows that it is *unwise* to frequently pronounce that question. And he does not pronounce it with Adeimantus.

Back in his central paragraph, after pronouncing the question himself, Strauss goes on:

> Other Socratic utterances might enable one to ascertain Socrates' answer, but they are of no use for ascertaining Adeimantus' answer and therewith for gauging how deep the agreement is which Socrates and Adeimantus achieve.

So Strauss points to Socrates' answer but does not give it. He leaves it to you to pursue that question, because he goes on here to what Socrates and Adeimantus agree on. There are various ways to pursue Socrates' answer. The easiest is to follow Strauss: he gives references for two such utterances in his Nietzsche essay. You can look them up to get a start on Socrates' answer: *Sophist* 216b5–6 refers to "a kind of refutative god" (the Stranger), and *Theaetetus* 151d1–2 says "They are far from knowing that no god is ill-disposed to human beings." Both references suggest something remarkable: *philosophers* are gods; and the context in Strauss's Nietzsche essay suggests just what that means, as we will see in my Nietzsche lectures.

But the important thing for us at the center of Strauss's essay on the *Republic* is this: Why does Socrates fail to pronounce that question in the *Republic* or give his answer? The reason is that Socrates has a different purpose in speaking with young Adeimantus. He has no intention of raising the question of *what a god is* because in the *Republic* he is doing what Strauss said he was doing: laying down laws for the gods. Socrates is legislating what a god is for tortured Adeimantus, a young man who thinks he knows what a god is but is critical of the *actions* of the gods in the stories he was raised to believe and is tempted not to believe them or not to trust the gods. What Socrates does is alter or modify the gods Adeimantus thinks he knows in order to make them more moral, make them more worthy of Adeimantus's respect and honor.

If we look away from Strauss's central paragraph to the paragraph just before the central paragraph, we see that Strauss spoke there of how the *philosopher* was first introduced into the *Republic*. He was introduced in a way that corrected Socrates' earlier view of the arts—of the doing and making that humans engage in. In the corrected view of the arts, there is a hierarchy of arts where "the highest art, the art directing all the other arts . . . will prove to be philosophy." So Strauss introduced that directing action of philosophy in the paragraph before his central paragraph. As an art, as a doing or making, philosophy is the highest or directing art; philosophy is the ruling art.

Plato himself put Socrates' famous statement that *the philosopher must rule* only later in his *Republic*. In fact Plato put that statement at the very center of the *Republic*. So what Strauss has done is move *Plato's* central statement to just before *his own* center. And it is very easy to see why Strauss did that: at the center of his essay on Plato's *Republic* Strauss shows just how what Plato put at the center of his *Republic* actually came about. At the center of his essay on the *Republic* Strauss shows how Socrates the philosopher actually ruled: a philosopher rules by laying down new laws for the gods; a philosopher rules by ruling the view of the gods that will rule the minds of the young men. If we look specifically to Adeimantus, we can say that the philosopher rules by ruling the minds of young men like him, who will welcome Socrates' reform of Homer's gods. Adeimantus stands for all noble young men rising to maturity in the crisis time in Athenian history when the very gods are mistrusted or doubted.

And Socrates' success in coming to rule the mind of Adeimantus and other young men like him points to Socrates' ultimate success: through Adeimantus and his like, Socrates' new legislation for the gods will rule the minds of all the boys and girls of the coming generations who will be raised in the views of their parents and who will continue to hold those views as grown-up citizens of the city. How the philosopher Socrates ruled—that is what Strauss put at the center of his essay on the *Republic*.

I turn now to general lessons from this central point.

Viewed *historically*—that is, looking at this event in the *Republic* against the background of the Greek past—we can say this: Homer and Hesiod, the founding Greek poets, the educators of Greece, were in their poetic way philosophic rulers through their gods and their heroes. But at the time of Plato's *Republic*, Homer's and Hesiod's gods were in crisis. Socrates in the *Republic* sets out to become a *philosophic ruler* during the crisis time of Homeric religion when Homer's gods were dying. That will be a theme of my first Plato lecture.

And viewed *historically* by looking backward from *Nietzsche's* perspective, we can say this: Socrates succeeded. Socrates became, as Nietzsche said, "the one turning point and vortex of so-called world history" (BT 15). That will be a theme of my Nietzsche lectures.

So, returning to Strauss's essay on Plato's *Republic*, we can see that at its center Strauss shows Socrates putting in place his *theological-political program*. And to quote Nietzsche again: since Plato, "all theologians and philosophers are on the same track" (BGE 191).

Now, in summary, I can say that this is part of what my coming five lectures will be about: the *theological-political programs* of the philosophers Plato and Nietzsche, what I call in my titles their *philosophic poetry*. But of course there is something of even greater importance than philosophic poetry, and my lectures will be about that as well. That more important matter is the *philosophy* that lies behind the theological-political programs, the understanding of *being* or *nature* that lies behind them or that generates them.

One way of looking at *philosophy itself* is this. In his final sentence of *The City and Man*, Strauss speaks of "the all-important question that is coeval with philosophy," the question, what is a god? That question is "*coeval*" with philosophy because it arises whenever and wherever philosophy arises. The reason it arises is that the question, What is a god?, is an *ontological* question, a question about *being*. It asks, what is the *highest possible being*? So while the question "What is a god?" has a practical dimension as it has in Socrates' discussion with Adeimantus, for a philosopher the essential dimension of the question is ontological, it is *theoretical* and not *practical*. It is a specific ontological question within the comprehensive ontological question; the comprehensive question asks, *What is the being of beings?*; a specific question within that question asks, *What is the highest being?*

So the two themes of the rest of my lectures are *philosophy* and *philosophic poetry* in Plato and Nietzsche. And my approach will be the approach of a reader: How does the distinction between the *exoteric* and the *esoteric* lead us to a proper understanding of *philosophy* and *philosophic poetry* in Plato and Nietzsche?

I want to end this first Strauss lecture on a point about Strauss. I focused on the central sentences of the central paragraph of his essay on the *Republic* not in order to demonstrate that Strauss too wrote exoterically. Of course he wrote exoterically. Instead, I focused on the central sentences of the central paragraph in order to show that what Strauss chose to treat at the center, *what a god is*, is not only an ontological question but becomes a part of a philosopher's legislation. We see from Strauss's central treatment of what a god is that legislating what a god is is in part an instrument in a philosopher's rule. Strauss shows that that is so with Plato, and I will show it is also so with Nietzsche.

Plato himself returned to the issue of *what a god is* in the last book of the *Republic*, Book 10, in which Socrates forces a return to the topic of poetry and a resolution of the "*ancient quarrel between philosophy and poetry*" (607b). The resolution of the quarrel is based on the natural superiority of the wise, that is, the naturally legitimate rule of the philosopher. As the natural ruler, the philosopher employs poetry. And Book 10 shows that the most striking aspect of that poetry is the philosopher's new teaching on the gods and on the soul. The teaching that Socrates puts forward in Book 10 continues his legislation about the gods and the soul: he makes the gods the moral judges of human behavior and he makes the soul immortal, living out its next life in reward and punishment for its actions in this life.

Part of the long story of Western philosophy must include a large chapter on how *disastrous* this new teaching by Platonic philosophers turned out to be in opening the way for Revelation or Christianity. I will say more on that in later lectures, but to end this lecture I will ignore that in order to end on a very fine phrase by Strauss describing this new Socratic legislation on the gods and the soul. He calls it "*ministerial poetry*," and both words are important. It is *poetry*, something made by human invention, human imagination. And that's where my titles on "*philosophic poetry*" come from.

In its origins this use of the word *poetry* is Plato's use, and I'll deal with that in my Plato lectures. But here Strauss makes it his own by adding the word *ministerial* as an adjective to modify *poetry*. It is the *perfect word* because it has a double sense, *political* and *social*, and both senses apply.

Strauss emphasizes the political: *ministerial* in this sense means in the service of the ruler or government; for instance, the *Minister* of Finance serves the ruling government. Plato's new ministerial poetry of gods and the soul is in the service of the new king, the philosopher ruler; the new ministerial poetry serves the interests of philosophy and that is its ultimate reason for existence. But the exclusivity of that first sense is modified and beautified by the second sense that Strauss does not mention.

The verb *minister* carries a secondary sense in English, a *social* or *therapeutic* sense of giving aid or service to those in need of it; one *ministers* to the sick or the wounded in order to ease their distress. And that too is what philosophic ministerial poetry does: the Socratic poetry of moral gods and immortal souls gives aid and comfort to those like Adeimantus who suffer spiritually from the loss of their beliefs in justice and in the gods. And Adeimantus stands for a whole generation that will be ministered to by the new Socratic poetry.

That's why I use the phrase *philosophic poetry* in my titles: *philosophy*, the drive to understand, comes to understand; and out of that understanding it generates or gives birth to a poetry that *ministers* to *its* interests while ministering as well to the larger civil community within which alone philosophy can prosper. So my lectures are about "Philosophy and Its Poetry." They are about the *philosophy* of Plato and of Nietzsche, and, I'll say right now and try to demonstrate in my lectures, the *philosophy* of Plato and Nietzsche seems to me to *converge* or to *share essentials* when Plato and Nietzsche are read as Strauss showed us how to read them. And my lectures are about the *philosophic poetry* of Plato and of Nietzsche and that poetry *diverges* radically or stands in warlike opposition, one against the other. And the divergence has reasons as good as the reason for the convergence regarding philosophy itself.

And finally my lectures are also about the *good reasons* for Nietzsche's opposition to Plato's philosophic poetry and why those reasons naturally turn *us* toward Nietzsche's philosophic poetry.

LECTURE 2

Strauss, Nietzsche, and the Philosophic Poetry of the Future

In my first lecture, I looked at Strauss's recovery of exoteric writing in his letters to Klein and then at a text by Strauss that showed how he too wrote exoterically and, more importantly, how he led his reader to the esoteric heart of Plato's exoteric book, the *Republic*.

In today's lecture, I look at a text by Strauss that shows that he wrote exoterically about Nietzsche too, and, more importantly, led his reader to the esoteric heart of Nietzsche's exoteric book, *Beyond Good and Evil*. Today's lecture is a commentary on parts of Strauss's late essay, "Note on the Plan of Nietzsche's *Beyond Good and Evil*." It was written from March, 1972–February, 1973; Strauss died seven months later, in September, 1973. Strauss arranged what he knew would be his last book, *Studies in Platonic Political Philosophy*, so that this essay on Nietzsche would occupy a special place in it. The book has a roughly chronological order from ancients through moderns, but Strauss planned that his Nietzsche essay would be placed out of order at the center, paired with "Jerusalem and Athens," which it follows. This is a *structurally* significant move for a thinker who took centering to be part of a careful author's art, and who himself constantly practiced the art of centering in beautiful ways. It is an even more significant *thematic* move: after the long, historically defining conflict of Jerusalem and Athens comes Nietzsche.

Strauss's lifelong study following his discovery of the exotericism of the philosophers was Platonic political philosophy. Nietzsche had been the philosopher who so dominated and charmed him from his twenty-second through his thirtieth year that he literally believed everything he understood of him. Although he ceased being simply dominated and charmed by Nietzsche in his thirtieth year, 1929, Strauss continued studying Nietzsche all his life. By putting his Nietzsche essay out of chronological order at the center of his last book, Strauss seems to be saying quietly: in the study of Platonic political philosophy, Nietzsche now occupies the central place, just after Jerusalem and Athens.

The opening of Strauss's essay: Nietzsche and Plato

Strauss opens his Nietzsche essay by singling out *Beyond Good and Evil* as Nietzsche's "most beautiful" book, and to clarify what he means he moves in his very first paragraph to Plato and Plato's books. From the very beginning, then, Strauss puts Nietzsche and Plato together. And he will put them together constantly throughout his essay, including at the very end.

In his third paragraph, Strauss notes that Nietzsche "presents himself as the antagonist of Plato," and he summarizes what he had said in his second paragraph about Nietzsche and his most beautiful book by again referring to Plato: he says *Beyond Good and Evil* is the book in which Nietzsche "'platonizes' as regards the 'form' more than anywhere else." Nietzsche's way of presenting his thoughts in this book *platonizes*, it resembles Plato's way of presenting *his* thoughts. Plato and Nietzsche are both exoteric writers who beautify their thoughts through what Strauss calls a "graceful subtlety as regards form, as regards intention, as regards the art of silence," crucial elements of the exoteric art: *form, intention,* and *an art of silence.*

Immediately after saying that, Strauss turns in his fourth paragraph to Nietzsche's preface to *Beyond Good and Evil,* specifically to Nietzsche the *antagonist* of Plato: "Plato's fundamental error was his invention of the pure mind and of the good in itself." Strauss then brings in Plato himself in order to make a very important point about *Plato's* artfulness in his invention of pure mind:

> From this premise one can easily be led to Diotima's conclusion that no human being is wise, but only the god is; human beings can only strive for wisdom or philosophize; gods do not philosophize.

Strauss thus moves from Nietzsche's *opposition* to Plato's invention of the pure mind and the good in itself to a *defense* of Plato that brings in the gods from a dialogue by Plato. That dialogue moves the pure mind out of human beings and locates it only in the gods. Plato is subtle: his "fundamental error" seems not to be a statement about human minds but only about the gods' minds—and what could *that* mean?

Strauss's defense of Plato through Plato's subtlety then leads him to jump from the preface of Nietzsche's book to its very end:

> In the penultimate aphorism of *Beyond Good and Evil* in which Nietzsche delineates 'the genius of the heart'—a super-Socrates who is in fact the god Dionysos—Nietzsche divulges after the proper preparation the novelty, suspect perhaps especially among philosophers, that gods too philosophize.

So is Plato *wrong* about the gods and their pure minds? Do the gods too philosophize as Nietzsche *divulges*? To divulge is to *reveal a secret*, perhaps a dangerous secret. If it is especially suspected among philosophers that gods philosophize, what about wise Diotima, Socrates' teacher in the *Symposium* who said they do not philosophize?

Strauss then does something he had learned to do very early as a careful reader: separate an author's *character*, a figure in a dialogue, from the author himself—he separates *Diotima* from *Plato* in order to make a most remarkable suggestion: "Plato could well have thought that gods philosophize (cf. *Sophist* 216b5–6, *Theaetetus* 151d1–2)." If you look up those two references you find that they suggest that the gods *do* philosophize—and more than that, they suggest that the gods who philosophize are the *philosophers themselves*.

So Strauss suggests that *Plato* held a different view from what he had his *Diotima* teach. But more importantly than that for us, Strauss, at the beginning of his Nietzsche essay, arranges or engineers a contrast between Nietzsche and his apparent *antagonist* Plato that forces us to think about whether Plato himself really held what Nietzsche said was his "fundamental error." Did Plato the philosopher make that error in his own thinking? Or did Plato the philosopher find it desirable to have his Diotima, Socrates' teacher, *teach* that view?

By setting up the contrast and then simply giving two references Strauss suggests to a reader who is paying attention that Plato *thought* what Nietzsche thought but found it desirable to *teach* something different through Diotima. And that suggests that Strauss thought that Nietzsche and his antagonist Plato really thought the same thing about the gods and philosophy, the difference being that Nietzsche divulged the secret about the gods philosophizing by introducing the philosophizing god Dionysos.

But Nietzsche himself suggested that "this novelty" was not entirely a novelty because it was "suspect perhaps especially among philosophers." Nietzsche may well know that the novelty he introduces is no novelty at all but a thing long known to philosophers, though covered up by philosophers like his antagonist Plato, who had his Diotima teach the opposite. So Nietzsche's platonizing, his "graceful subtlety as regards form . . . intention . . . [and] the art of silence," includes divulging about the gods what Plato also thought but did not divulge, or divulged only to a reader like Strauss who looks away from what Diotima taught to other passages in Plato to discover what Plato really thought.

So in his Nietzsche essay, Strauss almost begins—not by *divulging* secretive Plato's secret view but by subtly indicating that Plato knew the same truth Nietzsche knew but kept it secret while Nietzsche divulged it. By pointing to Plato's secret, Strauss points to a feature of Plato's own platonizing in a context where he is examining Nietzsche's platonizing. And by pointing to Plato's secret, Strauss suggests that Diotima tells a *noble lie* about the gods that serves Plato's political purpose for philosophy. And Nietzsche, Strauss may also suggest, divulged that secret in order to serve *his* political purpose for philosophy.

And here I draw a conclusion that only the rest of my lectures can show to be valid: Plato and Nietzsche platonize for the same reason, the well-being of philosophy; they platonize in the service of philosophy. Their difference in keeping secret and divulging—on the matter of the gods and philosophy!—can be traced to the same reason: each interpreted the spiritual situation of their times and each taught what the times required for the well-being of philosophy.

Strauss contrasts Nietzsche and Plato throughout his essay, but because we don't have time to consider all of those occasions, I jump to the very end of Strauss's essay with *its* contrast of Nietzsche and Plato. The issue is no longer the gods but the virtues, a crucial matter of morality, one of the themes of the second main part of Nietzsche's book. The specific issue is the virtues as part of "the philosophy of the future" to which, Nietzsche said, *Beyond Good and Evil* is a "prelude." In particular, the issue is "the virtues of the philosopher of the future." Strauss brings in Plato by saying that those virtues "differ from the Platonic virtues." In Strauss's example two of the Platonic virtues are replaced by two modern virtues. And the last sentences of his essay say: "This is one illustration among many of what [Nietzsche] means by characterizing nature by its 'Vornehmheit' (aph. 188). *Die vornehme Natur ersetzt die göttliche Natur.*"

And that's the end. Strauss ends his English essay with a German sentence. He hides his meaning in a foreign language, Nietzsche's language. The sentence says "*Noble nature replaces divine nature.*" That is, nature as Nietzsche taught it, noble nature, replaces nature as Plato taught it, nature and the super-natural that transcends it. Does Strauss mean to *endorse* that replacement? Does Strauss's essay-long contrast between Nietzsche and Plato end on his own veiled recommendation of Nietzsche's teaching on nature as replacing Plato's teaching on nature? Strauss left it veiled. So, for now at least, we can leave it veiled.

I want to end this first part of this lecture on another aspect of Strauss's contrast between Plato and Nietzsche on *platonizing*. Toward the beginning of his essay, Strauss calls attention to the overall structure Nietzsche gave his book, its "plan" as divided into nine chapters. Strauss emphasizes that Chapters 1 and 2 are on philosophy and Chapter 3 is on religion and that these three chapters are separated from the later chapters by a chapter of "about 123 'Sayings and Interludes.'" This separating chapter divides the book into two main parts. Strauss's conclusion about this form Nietzsche gave his book is that "Philosophy and religion, it seems, belong together." Part of Nietzsche's platonizing as regards form puts philosophy and religion together and separates them from morals and politics; Nietzsche separates the two most important things from the also important things. Now I can turn to just *how* philosophy and religion belong together for Nietzsche.

Nietzsche's philosophy chapters

Chapter One of *Beyond Good and Evil* is "On the Prejudices of the Philosophers": it criticizes those prejudices in order to free the mind from them. Chapter Two, "The Free Mind," is also on philosophy, and it sets out what a free mind can attain, what Nietzsche's free mind has already attained. Part of the platonizing form of Chapter Two is that Nietzsche gave it a meaningful center.

Strauss begins his first paragraph on the philosophy chapters with this sentence: "Nietzsche says very little about religion in the first two chapters." Of course he does: these are the chapters on *philosophy*. Strauss's sentence makes it clear that his interest here is *religion*, religion's presence in the philosophy chapters. Strauss's ultimate interest is of course philosophy. But this is a writing by Strauss and *its* chief interest is religion in the philosopher Nietzsche, Nietzsche's theological-political program or his *philosophic poetry* in its aspect as religion. Strauss's next sentences say:

> One could say that he speaks there on religion only in a single aphorism which happens to be the shortest (37). That aphorism is a kind of corollary to the immediately preceding one in which he sets forth in the most straightforward and unambiguous manner that is compatible with his intention, the particular character of his fundamental proposition according to which life is will to power or seen from within the world is will to power and nothing else.

Notice: Strauss says "a single aphorism" on religion and that single aphorism is "a kind of corollary" or consequence of the preceding aphorism, which contains Nietzsche's *fundamental proposition*. Notice too that Strauss suggests that Nietzsche "sets forth" his "fundamental proposition" in a manner that is not completely straightforward or unambiguous: Nietzsche is not completely open with his fundamental proposition; he has a particular intention in the way he sets it out. But Strauss's main point is at the end: Nietzsche's "fundamental proposition" concerns *life* in Nietzsche's sense, and life in that sense is simply "the world," the whole of things. We would say, in the language of philosophy that Nietzsche refuses to use, that his fundamental proposition concerns *being as such*; it is an *ontology*, a statement about the nature or character of beings as a whole: "seen from within," seen the way we can never actually see it, "the world is will to power and nothing else." Strauss is clear: *will to power* is Nietzsche's name for the being of beings, the nature of nature.

Strauss then connects Nietzsche's ontology with Plato's ontology:

> The will to power takes the place which the *eros*—the striving for "the good in itself"—occupies in Plato's thought.

Strauss's definition of *eros* here, *the good in itself*, is part of what he had said was Nietzsche's view of Plato's fundamental error. For me that shows Strauss's intention: he has no intention of setting out the relation between Nietzsche's ontology and Plato's ontology in a completely straightforward or unambiguous manner; he keeps that relation somewhat more ambiguous than it actually is.

Strauss goes on in the paragraph to touch on an issue that lies behind the whole history of exoteric teachings in philosophy, the recognition by philosophers that the truths they discover are dangerous, and Strauss uses Nietzsche's word for that, "*deadly.*" Both will to power and *eros* give expression to a truth about reality that is *deadly*. As Seth Benardete said to begin his account of *eros* in Plato's *Symposium*: "The truth about Eros is terrifying." What does Nietzsche do with the fundamental truth that he regarded as deadly? He says this:

> Nietzsche's statements or suggestions are deliberately enigmatic (aph. 40). By suggesting or saying that the truth is deadly, he does his best to break the power of deadly truth; he suggests that the most important, the most comprehensive truth—the truth regarding all truths—is life-giving.

"*Deliberately enigmatic*": Nietzsche is obscure on purpose, obscure in order to suggest something; "*aph. 40*" speaks about the necessity of masks for everything "profound." What is *deliberately enigmatic* about saying that "the most comprehensive truth" is *deadly*? Strauss says that it is Nietzsche's way of beginning to *break* its deadly power. This is crucial. The comprehensive truth at first *looks* deadly, but it is actually *life-giving*. Seen correctly, what looks deadly is life-giving. And Strauss will show that Nietzsche does exactly that in the passage that will say it only once: Nietzsche shows how what appears deadly is in fact the opposite. That is coming as the main point of my lecture.

To get to that point, Strauss treats another aspect of Nietzsche's platonizing as regards form: the *structure* he gave to his series of aphorisms. Nietzsche arranged the series with great care, as Strauss shows by calling attention to the central aphorisms of this chapter on the free mind:

> The connection between aphorism 34 and 35 is a particularly striking example of the lucid, if somewhat hidden, order governing the sequence of aphorisms: the desultory character of Nietzsche's argument is more pretended than real.

What looks *desultory*, or seems to lack a definite plan or purpose, is in fact *lucid* or clear if *somewhat hidden*. Why pretend there is no plan or purpose when there is a plan or purpose? Strauss does not say, but it's obvious and frequent in Nietzsche: pretending there is no plan or purpose allows you to *notice* a plan and then to work to discover the *purpose* of the plan. *You* discover it, *you* make it your own: you realize Nietzsche is teaching you.

Strauss's next paragraph begins with this: "We can now turn to the two aphorisms in BGE I-II that can be said to be devoted to religion (36–37)." We can now turn to what Strauss had said was *one paragraph* devoted to religion but now says is *two paragraphs* devoted to religion. He will correct himself by returning to one paragraph, but to say *two* makes you look for a reason to say it, and the reason seems to be the connection between the religion aphorism and the one just before it, a connection that reflects the connection between 34 and 35 and is of high importance: "Aphorism 36 presents the reasoning in support of the doctrine of the will to power."

Aphorism 36 is *reasoning*; it is philosophy. Aphorism 37 is only *a kind of corollary* because it follows the reasoning with something that is not reasoning but that belongs to religion. Strauss does not repeat the reasoning of section 36. Instead, he judges it, assigning it very high praise indeed: it combines "what is at the same time the most intransigent intellectual probity and the most bewitching playfulness." The reasoning combines the strictest philosophical logical seriousness and play. The intellectual probity of the reasoning of section 36 pursues strictly logical inference about what the mind can know of the self, the other, and the world as a whole. The reasoning of section 36 draws the conclusion that the world, the totality, seen from inside, would be will to power and nothing else. The most bewitching playfulness follows in section 37, where the reasoning triggers horror in Nietzsche's "friends" and indispensable help that Nietzsche offers his friends. The reasoning and the play are a pinnacle of philosophic communication on the fundamental matters.

I will look at the reasoning in my last Nietzsche lecture. Here I want to call attention only to Strauss's emphasis that aphorism 36 is philosophic method applied to nature as a whole. In his philosophy chapters, Nietzsche leads his reader to a comprehensive rational conclusion about the nature of nature, about what philosophy ultimately seeks. Strauss sets that out even more briefly than Nietzsche did, because he has already told us that his essay is concerned with *religion* in *Beyond Good and Evil*. Religion cannot be more important than philosophy, but Strauss chose to focus on religion, that is, on philosophic poetry. After the reasoning comes the kind of corollary or inference. Strauss shows that that corollary is what the reasoning draws out of the audience that hears it, draws out of the free minds that Nietzsche is training. The free minds respond to the reasoning but not with more reasoning, not with *philosophy*, but with a deeply human reaction to philosophy's rational conclusion, the response Nietzsche anticipates even from his best-prepared, free-minded friends.

So we move to Strauss's paragraph 9, to the "kind of corollary" to Nietzsche's "fundamental proposition": "After having tempted some of his readers (cf. aph. 30) with the doctrine of the will to power Nietzsche makes them raise the question as to whether that doctrine does not assert, to speak popularly, that God is refuted but the devil is not."

Which readers does Nietzsche tempt by forcing them to raise that question? Strauss quotes Nietzsche's answer next; it is addressed to "my friends"—Nietzsche tempts his "friends," the free minds, those he makes his friends by what he teaches them. But here they face a serious problem. By saying "(cf. aph. 30)," Strauss suggests that we should think of Nietzsche's readers with the distinction in mind that Nietzsche made in aphorism 30, his only explicit reference to the exoteric and the esoteric. If you do what Strauss says and read aph. 30, you see that Nietzsche says that the philosopher's "highest insights" will sound foolish and sometimes like crimes when they come to the ears of "those who are not the kind for them." In section 37 Nietzsche suggests that even his potential friends, those who *are* the kind for it, will hear the highest insight of his reasoning in the way aphorism 30 says: they will judge, that's *madness*; that's *criminal*. Nietzsche says that his friends *speak popularly* in speaking of God and the devil. But his friends are the free minds; they do not believe in God or the devil. But as modern free minds they no longer have a language that can state strongly enough just how *criminal* they find Nietzsche's conclusion. So they adopt the old language, the popular language, for a moment and use *its* extremes, God and devil, to express their shock at his crime.

Having only paraphrased what Nietzsche's friends say, Strauss *quotes* what Nietzsche himself says: "He replies 'On the contrary! On the contrary, my friends! And, to the devil, what forces you to speak popularly?'"

Nietzsche is emphatic, repeating "On the contrary!" But he does not explain what the "contrary" is, nor does Strauss. So the reader has to think it out for himself. It's not hard. The contrary to "God is refuted" is "the devil is refuted." The transcendent God of Christian theology is what Nietzsche's friends think of as God; they are post-Christian atheists whose only concept of God is the Christian God. And if it's true that the totality of the world is will to power and nothing else, there is nothing beyond the world different from the world. Nietzsche's reasoning refutes a transcendent God. But the transcendent God of Christianity had condemned the world as the kingdom of darkness, as the place of the devil from which he would redeem us. So the contrary that Nietzsche's friends must think is that *that* God, the refuted God, is the *devil*, the refuted devil. Nietzsche invites his friends to think the greatest blasphemy. When they do what Nietzsche suggests and think the contrary, they think on their own the great blasphemy that Nietzsche himself does not pronounce. Strauss noted a similar technique in

Machiavelli and gave the reason for it: it forces the reader to become Machiavelli's *accomplice*, the reader thinks the shocking thought.

The other half of Nietzsche's "On the contrary!" is the great lesson in theology that Nietzsche teaches his Christian-atheist, free-minded friends: the contrary to "the devil is not [refuted]," is "God is not." Nietzsche thus suggests that his will to power view has a place for God, or for *gods*, as we will see. Nietzsche's friends must broaden their thinking about God or gods.

After we think through the two contraries as both Nietzsche and Strauss silently invite us to do, we come in Strauss's translation to: "And to the devil, what forces you to speak popularly?" Nietzsche's German word that Strauss translates "what" is *wer* or *who*: Nietzsche asks "*who* forces you?" That's important, because there is an implied answer to *who* forces you: Nietzsche's friends do not believe in God or the devil. So the *who* forcing them to "speak popularly" of God and the devil must be *the dead God* himself. The transcendent God is dead but not *gone*. The dead God still defines even for Nietzsche's free-minded friends *what a God is*. The two-thousand-year-old tradition is still powerful in its late atheists—when they think of "God" they think only of *that* God, the dead God, still powerful as their only idea of God. If the will to power view does *not refute God*, then Nietzsche's friends are going to have to start thinking differently about what a god is.

So the combination of reasoning and play in sections 36 and 37 allows Strauss to end this key little paragraph by saying, "The doctrine of the will to power—the whole doctrine of *Beyond Good and Evil*—is in a manner a vindication of God."

Nietzsche's ontology, his view of the world seen from the inside, *vindicates God*, as Strauss says and says five times. Nietzsche's ontology introduces a new way to think about divinity, about what a god is. Strauss has led his reader into the heart of this *temptation* by Nietzsche. The philosopher Nietzsche, having thought about what a god is, will offer a new teaching on the gods. That new teaching may not be all that new: at the beginning of his Nietzsche essay, Strauss had suggested that Nietzsche and Plato may not differ on what a god is, that the "super-Socrates," the philosophizing god Dionysos, may represent a shared view of what a god is. We can leave that issue for a moment and ask instead:

Why would Nietzsche *vindicate* God, why would he free God from blame or justify God? Even if "God" now means something entirely different from the transcendent God, why not just be atheist? Strauss answers that question without ever asking it directly: he ends his paragraph saying: "(Cf. aph. 150 and 295, as well as *Genealogy of Morals*, Preface Nr. 7)."

Strauss refers to aphorism 150 later to suggest that for Nietzsche there can be no livable "world" for humans without gods. Nietzsche seems to agree with Plato and the philosophic tradition that gods are necessary for a healthy social order. As for "aph. 295," it is the long aphorism that Strauss had already quoted on the "super-Socrates" who is in fact the god Dionysos. And Strauss's other reference, "*Genealogy of Morals* Pref. No. 7," speaks of a new complication and possibility for "the Dionysian drama of the 'Destiny of the Soul'" and of Dionysos himself as taking advantage of that new possibility, he, "the great old eternal comic poet of our existence!" In keeping with that reference, Strauss opens his account of the religion chapter as Nietzsche opened that chapter, on "the whole history of the soul hitherto"—for Nietzsche, the history of religion offers a history of the human soul at the point of a new complication and possibility for the human soul, perhaps in some way connected to the super-Socrates Dionysos.

Strauss ends his account of the philosophy chapters in *Beyond Good and Evil* on the one aphorism on religion in those chapters. He ends his treatment of philosophy with Nietzsche's invitation to his philosophically inclined friends to think differently about what a god is, to think about divinity free of Biblical transcendence, to think of divinity in connection with the fundamental proposition, to think of the implications of the will to power ontology for God or gods. More specifically, Strauss ends his account of philosophy saying that the ultimate conclusion of philosophy's reasoning, the world is will to power and nothing else, is a vindication of God, and he adds three references to help you think about a new view of the gods. Perhaps Nietzsche's *philosophy* can generate a new view of the gods, a new poetry of divinity for humans whose world can turn only around a god. After suggesting that promise of Nietzsche's *philosophy* for religion, Strauss moves directly to Nietzsche's chapter on religion.

Nietzsche's religion chapter

Strauss first lays out *the plan* of the religion chapter: it deals with religion up till now and the religion of the future and religion as a whole. Strauss treats in greatest detail the series of aphorisms that deal with religion today and in the future. Nietzsche treats religion today in aphorisms 53 and 54, the central two of his chapter; one is on *atheism* today, the other is on *the assassination of the soul* today. Contemporary thought rejects these two central Christian teachings on God and the soul. The next aphorism, 55, deals with the consequence of today's atheism and soul-assassination as something far worse even than Christianity: modern nihilism, though neither Nietzsche nor Strauss uses the word *nihilism*. Strauss treats the step after nihilism in a separate paragraph.

> Nietzsche does not mean to sacrifice God for the sake of the Nothing, for while recognizing the deadly truth that God died he aims at transforming it into a life-inspiring one or rather to discover in the depth of the deadly truth its opposite.

Strauss says "*aims at transforming it*"—but he knows that's wrong, that's not what Nietzsche did, and he corrects himself: "or rather" Nietzsche *discovers* the opposite, discovers an unexpected fact—nothing needs to be transformed; instead, Nietzsche discovers the opposite to deadly truth. So the movement here is similar to what Strauss had said earlier about Nietzsche's "deliberately enigmatic" statements: what first appears deadly is in truth "life-giving." Strauss then turns to aphorism 56, the one directly after the nihilism aphorism. He paraphrases, quotes, and comments on this most important aphorism in the religion chapter, the single aphorism on eternal return.

> But Nietzsche, prompted by "some enigmatic desire," has tried for a long time to penetrate pessimism to its depth. . . . He thus has grasped a more world-denying way of thinking than that of any previous pessimist.

The "enigmatic desire" can only be *the passion to know* that has driven Nietzsche in his inquiry. Penetrating pessimism to its depth, Nietzsche arrives at what seems to be the most world-denying way of thinking, the way of thinking that views the world as will to power and nothing else—to which his friends first reacted as horrifyingly world denying.

> Yet a man who has taken this road has perhaps without intending to do this opened his eyes to the opposite ideal—to the ideal belonging to the religion of the future.

That's exactly what Nietzsche says: "opened his eyes to the opposite ideal." That ideal is the eternal return of everything that is, and it is important that both Nietzsche and Strauss call it an *ideal.* But why add that ambiguous "*perhaps*" that could mean *perhaps without intending to do so*? Strauss's next sentence explains the *perhaps* as Nietzsche did not:

"It goes without saying that what in some other men was 'perhaps' the case was a fact in Nietzsche's thought and life." No, it does not "go without saying," it has to be said and Strauss has to say it, because some of his followers maintained that Nietzsche was fundamentally *looking for* a new ideal, that Nietzsche was most basically a religious teacher in search of a new ideal to counter the absence of ideals in our now nihilistic culture. Strauss says with this clarification of *perhaps* what Nietzsche himself said: he did not *mean* to discover a new ideal, he discovered it "without actually meaning to do so."

So again Strauss corrects himself, as he did with *transform* and *discover,* and both corrections say the same thing: Nietzsche is a *philosopher,* not a *religious thinker.* Nietzsche's thought and life intended one thing: to discover the true. He did not *intend* to find a new ideal; instead, he found a new ideal as a consequence of his passion for the truth, as a consequence of his discovery that the world is will to power and nothing else. That discovery had as an unintended consequence his glimpsing a new ideal. This is the important sequence that allowed Nietzsche to move from philosophy to religion: his discovery of the truth opened his eyes on a new ideal; philosophy led to philosophic poetry. As Strauss says,

> The adoration of the Nothing proves to be the indispensable transition from every kind of world-denial to the most unbounded Yes: the eternal Yes-saying to everything that was and is.

The unexpected insight of the truth-seeker who thinks nihilism to its depth is the new ideal that the world as it is returns *just as it is* an infinite number of times. Strauss goes on in his paragraph to make some interesting comments about that ideal that I have omitted; he then quotes the end of the aphorism:

> "And this," Nietzsche concludes his suggestion regarding eternal repetition of what was and is, "would not be *circulus vitiosus deus*?"

The Latin phrase is ambiguous, as Strauss notes: A vicious circle made god? God is a vicious circle? Strauss makes two important comments. First, "[Nietzsche's] atheism is not unambiguous, for he had doubts whether there can be a world, any world whose center is not God (aph. 150)." There it is again, aph. 150, which Nietzsche seems to have made the central aphorism of *Beyond Good and Evil*. It suggests, Strauss indicates, that only around a god can things become a world; the human world, the *lived world*, the cultural world as a place of meaning and significance, is possible only with god or gods. Nietzsche's atheism is ambiguous because he suggests that gods are necessary, socially necessary, necessary for there to be a cultural world.

Second,

> The conclusion of the present aphorism [56] reminds us, through its form, of the theological aphorism occurring in the first two chapters (37) where Nietzsche brings out the fact that in a manner the doctrine of the will to power is a vindication of God, if a decidedly non-theistic vindication of God.

(Note incidentally that Strauss returns to his true judgment: *the* theological aphorism in the philosophy chapters, *the one*, is 37, his friends' mistaken reaction to his will to power view that God is refuted but the devil is not.) Strauss restated the end of aphorism 56: would eternal return "not be *circulus vitiosus deus*?" If that "reminds us" of aphorism 37 then *we* have to add something; we have to say what Nietzsche said in 37: "On the contrary! On the contrary, my friends." The contrary here is that eternal return is not a *vicious* circle but, on the contrary, the *virtuous* circle of life made eternal, made god in some sense. Eternal return is the making divine of the whole natural cycle of things. Eternal return is a non-theistic vindication of God.

So Strauss leads his reader to see that in aphorism 56 Nietzsche shows his friends the *genuine response* to understanding the world as will to power and nothing else. The will to power view does not *refute* God but instead leads to a new ideal, even to a new conception of divinity.

I said in my 1996 book, *Leo Strauss and Nietzsche*, that this insight into the connection between will to power and eternal return, between philosophy and religion, is Strauss's greatest contribution to Nietzsche studies. It is an *exegetical* contribution, the contribution of a most exceptional reader with lifelong experience in reading Platonic political philosophers. Strauss shows that *he* is the reader Nietzsche wants; *he* gives the proper interpretation to the two most important conclusions in *Beyond Good and Evil*. First comes *philosophy's* deepest insight: to be is to be will to power and nothing else. Second comes its corollary for *religion*: the new view of *what is* leads to a new highest ideal, the affirmation of the world as it is, and it leads to a vindication of god, of what alone can make a world possible for humans.

Strauss saw the inner coherence of Nietzsche's thinking as Nietzsche laid it out in the first three chapters of *Beyond Good and Evil*. That inner coherence is the deepest *platonizing* in Nietzsche: that is, in Nietzsche as in Plato, philosophy at its deepest *generates* or *gives birth to* a political philosophy or philosophic poetry in the form of a theological-political program. This is the ultimate way that Nietzsche is a *Platonic political philosopher*, a philosopher who succeeded in doing what Plato did. First comes the *esoteric insight* into the world reserved for the philosopher, wholly a matter for the intellect. Then comes *an exoteric teaching* for all, a teaching founded on the human passions that makes a mere totality into a world, a livable world for human communities.

My Plato lectures will treat both these matters in Plato: Plato's account of *philosophy's deepest insight* into *eros*, and Plato's account of *philosophic poetry*, the *platonism* that was the result of Plato's understanding of the spiritual situation of his time, the platonism that came to dominate Western philosophy. And my Nietzsche lectures will treat both these matters in Nietzsche: Nietzsche's *philosophic insight* into will to power as the fundamental fact, and Nietzsche's *philosophic poetry* as reasoned opposition to Plato's platonism that was the result of Nietzsche's understanding of the spiritual situation of our time.

I want to quote one last statement from Strauss's account of Nietzsche's religion chapter:

> There is an important ingredient, not to say the nerve, of Nietzsche's 'theology' of which I have not spoken and shall not speak since I have no access to it.

This is emphatic, this is vehement—it is Strauss's adamant refusal to speak. I want to speak about that, but I will wait until my Nietzsche lectures to speak about *the nerve* of Nietzsche's theology as his actual reintroduction of gods, of what he seems to regard as necessary to make a world. But now, to end my Strauss lectures, I want to move to the most important point in his treatment of Nietzsche's chapters on morals and politics.

Nietzsche's chapters on morals and politics

Strauss has shown that in Nietzsche philosophy generates a new highest ideal as philosophic poetry. But Strauss also shows that in Nietzsche, philosophy generates a program for *morality*, a new good and bad that is fundamentally different from the good and evil of Platonism. Here, I will deal with only one point in Strauss's treatment of morals and politics. It arises at the end of his account of the chapter "Our Virtues," where he shows how a new teaching on human virtue arises out of Nietzsche's new understanding of nature. Strauss emphasizes that Nietzsche the philosopher aimed to see again "the terrible basic text of homo natura," of human nature, the "eternal basic text," as Nietzsche called it. And Nietzsche went beyond *seeing* human nature, to *act* on what he *saw*. His action concerns how "man is to be 'retranslated into nature,'" how man can be "made natural" after thousands of years of moral thinking according to which humanity is in some way both subnatural and supernatural.

So we get to Strauss's paragraph 35, the most important paragraph of this part of Strauss's essay, where he speaks of ". . . an order of rank of the natures; at the summit of the hierarchy is the complementary man." Nietzsche says *complementary man* once in *Beyond Good and Evil.* Strauss says it five times. It is Nietzsche's name for *the philosopher* at this point in human history, the philosopher as thinker and actor. Strauss has some remarkable things to say about the complementary man that I have to omit. But the following sentence may be Strauss's most thought-provoking sentence in the essay: "His supremacy [the supremacy of the complementary man] is shown by the fact that he solves the highest, the most difficult problem."

Strauss is very careful with his words. He does not say, *aims* to solve the highest, the most difficult problem or *tries* to solve it. He says *solves* it. What is that problem? Strauss states it as *the problem of late modern times*, the problem facing a philosopher who lives in the maturity of modern times when *the ideal* that rules modern times has itself become the problem.

I have to say one thing about modern times that my six lectures do not give me space to enlarge in detail. *Modern times* are the times of the *technological mastery of nature* based on the *scientific understanding of nature.* That revolutionary way of thinking and acting did not just happen; it was the result of concerted work by *philosophers* who judged it to be necessary—this is one of the most important events in Western history and in global history. It is an amazing chapter in the history of Western philosophy when the foundation of modern times is laid by philosophers of whom the most important seem to me to be Francis Bacon and René Descartes.

They judged it necessary to launch the view whose problematic outcome is what Strauss here addresses. I will expand a bit on that at the end of this lecture.

Strauss defines the problem in his next two sentences:

> As we have observed, for Nietzsche nature has become a problem and yet he cannot do without nature. Nature, we may say, has become a problem owing to the fact that man is conquering nature and there are no assignable limits to that conquest.

Our common understanding of the problem of the conquest of nature is the problem of modern technological science in its effort to master nature: the ecological disasters that the attempted mastery of nature can generate. But here, Strauss follows Nietzsche in identifying the problem differently. The problem of "no assignable limits" to the conquest of nature is the problem of the conquest of *human nature*, a conquest that is the direct result of *modern virtue*.

Strauss identifies the problem: "As a consequence, people have come to think of abolishing suffering and inequality."

These are the two chief features of modern virtue according to Nietzsche: the *abolition of suffering* and *equality of rights*. As Nietzsche showed, they are the modern, secular version of Christian virtue. They pose the fundamental problem for Nietzsche for one reason only, the reason Strauss identifies: "Yet suffering and inequality are the prerequisites of human greatness (aph. 239 and 257)." The greatness that matters most is the greatest human greatness, philosophy itself, the attainment of insight by the highest human spirituality, and the necessary action that that insight alone can see to be necessary. Strauss's point is Nietzsche's point: the limitless conquest of nature threatens to bring about the *end of philosophy*.

Strauss then turns to *Thus Spoke Zarathustra* to build on what he had said earlier. I have to omit that, because I haven't discussed the earlier points. But for us it is enough to read the end of the paragraph. Strauss's last sentence says this: "Nature, the eternity of nature, owes its being to a postulation, to an act of the will to power on the part of the highest nature." Strauss's wording ties Nietzsche's act of solving the highest, the most difficult problem to similar acts by the great philosophers across the history of philosophy. The key word is *postulation*—it means to *posit something as true* or to *claim that something is true*. To *postulate* something as true is what all the great legislative philosophers have done. The actions of the highest natures, the history-making philosophers, postulate as true what they see as beneficial to philosophy and humanity in their times. What begins as a philosopher's legislative postulations comes to be lived as true by the social order that gradually embraces them. Such postulations by the philosophers are all what Strauss says Nietzsche's postulation is: acts of the will to power on the part of the highest natures.

Strauss says Nietzsche's act of *postulation* concerns the eternity of nature, the eternal return of nature. He does not say at the end what he had already said at the start: Nietzsche's postulation of eternal return solves the highest, most difficult problem of the conquest of nature that knows no assignable limits. *Just how* does Nietzsche's postulation solve that problem? Strauss does not say directly, but the whole drift of what his essay has been saying provides the answer, Nietzsche's answer. The doctrine of eternal return solves the highest problem because it is a *preservative* teaching, the ultimate *conservatism*, as Strauss says somewhat ironically.

Eternal return is not fundamentally a cosmological proposition; it is not fundamentally a *description* of the way the world is, although it may be lived that way by most people. Instead, all of Nietzsche's accounts of eternal return agree that it a statement of *desire*, the desire of a lover: the lover says to *the world as it is*, the totality as it naturally is, *that's* what I want and I want it an infinite number of times just as it is. It may be trivializing to say it, but it is the love of that lover that assigns limits to the conquest of nature, *beloved* nature. Beloved nature, beginning with beloved human nature, is not to be conquered through alteration but celebrated as it is. That trivial-sounding solution is in fact profound and wholly non-Romantic, based as it is on Nietzsche's analysis of the human passions and in particular on his analysis of the passion for *revenge* and the ways in which that passion has won historical supremacy and grounded our view of good and bad.

Strauss's essay on Nietzsche almost ends on the argument he makes that the complementary man solves the highest, most difficult problem. I take this to be one of Strauss's most important insights into Nietzsche. It is an insight into an aspect of Nietzsche's thinking that I have spelled out in my books on Nietzsche. From my first book on I have argued that Nietzsche's philosophy is *the first comprehensive ecological philosophy*, the philosophy whose moral imperative is the one that Nietzsche's Zarathustra announced at his beginning: "Be true to the earth!" or "Be loyal to the earth!"

That's almost where Strauss ends his essay, and that is where I end my Strauss lectures. The complementary man *solves* the highest, the most difficult problem. I find that breathtaking. For me, there is no stronger *endorsement* of

Nietzsche than that. Nietzsche *solves* the highest, most difficult problem of late modern times, the problem of assigning limits to the conquest of nature. Of all the things I find wonderful in Strauss, I find nothing more wonderful than that.

That ends my Strauss lectures, but Strauss will continue to be present throughout the rest of my lectures. The distinction between the *exoteric* and the *esoteric* that Strauss recovered in the history of philosophy will be present in my lectures on Plato and Nietzsche as the distinction both draw between *philosophy* and its *poetry*.

With Plato, Strauss showed how to read Plato in a new way that is actually the old way, the classical way. That way of reading recovers the genuine Plato, the Plato that Strauss said was "nearest my heart." I will use Strauss in aid of my main topic in Plato, a theme that Strauss noticed but did not develop himself: *How Socrates became Socrates*, the double story of how Socrates became the philosopher and political philosopher who Nietzsche said was the one turning point and vortex of so-called world history.

With Nietzsche, I will use Strauss more directly, but my main point will be one that Strauss did not develop: *How Nietzsche became Nietzsche*, the story of Nietzsche's becoming himself that he thought it was necessary for him to tell. I will use Nietzsche's autobiographical remarks to trace his becoming, but mostly I will look closely at a private notebook in which Nietzsche's becoming is displayed involuntarily in the chronological order of his notebook entries.

So my Plato and Nietzsche lectures look to the beginning of the *ancient* or *classical* tradition and to the other extreme, the end of the *modern* tradition in our time. And Strauss, I will show, provides indispensable aid for those extremes in what I called in my second book, *Nietzsche and Modern Times*, "the new history of philosophy made possible by Friedrich Nietzsche." That new history, aided by Strauss, can show that philosophy took a new turn with Plato or Socrates, a turn that ended with Nietzsche's conscious, anti-platonic turn to a new way. That new history of philosophy necessarily highlights a transition point between the two extremes of Plato and Nietzsche that I will not be able to treat in any detail in these lectures. That turning point is the founding of the modern world by philosophers fully aware of what they were doing and why they were doing it. I will say only a few words about it here.

The founding of the modern world

The founding of the modern world in Western Europe is the great event in philosophy and philosophy's poetry that still surrounds us, the wave that still "bears us today," as Strauss said. That European event has become a global event, as its founders knew it would. It was a *philosophic* event in which the greatest philosophers of the time united to defeat the common enemy and to secure rule for philosophy. Strauss showed that Machiavelli is the initial great founder of modern philosophy, and his book *Thoughts on Machiavelli* is probably his greatest book.

I don't dispute the singular importance of Machiavelli, but for me, the modern founding is most associated with Francis Bacon and René Descartes, two philosophic followers of Machiavelli. They are the masters whose exoteric writings led to the establishment and advancement of the scientific and technological view of nature. Like the philosophers before them to whom they pay credit, Machiavelli and Montaigne, and the philosophers after them who learned from them, Hobbes and Spinoza and the rest, they fought what Strauss too called "*the kingdom of darkness*," Christianity. And they succeeded in taming it. In my view, Bacon and Descartes tamed Christianity with their philosophic poetry, their modification of Christianity's *otherworldly* promises into *worldly* promises promising a paradise at the end of history through a scientific technology applied to nature. Their conscious secularization of the Christian dream gradually re-focused European dreaming on worldly rather than heavenly ends; they succeeded thereby in *taming* Christianity, a ruling religion whose warring fanaticism in their time cost Europe the Renaissance; their philosophic founding launched the modern view of nature and of human goals. It is a complex and wonderful story, and I tried to do justice to Bacon's and Descartes's part in it in my book, *Nietzsche and Modern Times*, a book that also argued that Nietzsche embraced the *scientific* aspects of the modern revolution while modifying or assigning limits to its *technological* aspects.

The exoteric, public teaching of Bacon and Descartes still stamps our time, a time now defined by the conquest of nature and what Strauss identified as the highest, most difficult problem, that man is conquering nature and there are no assignable limits to that conquest. A full assessment of Nietzsche's political program for philosophy would require a detailed study of the early modern philosophic founding and how it responded to religious rule over philosophy made possible in the West by Platonism, made actual by Christianity.

I will say one thing more about that great modern turning point. Descartes long contemplated just how he could best *mount the stage*, as he said, how he could best begin his part in the great modern fight to reestablish philosophy against ruling religion. He experimented with many different ways of mounting the stage and finally chose one way, the way he took in his first book, published when he was forty years old and already well known across Europe as a mathematical and scientific genius. His book begins with a six-part *autobiography*, his *Discourse on the Method*, which he calls a "*history*" of his becoming himself that he invites you to think of as a *fable*. In that *fabulous history*, Descartes shows himself *becoming a philosopher* and then necessarily becoming a *philosophic poet* whose poetry, whose permission for dreaming, would advance Francis Bacon's poetry on behalf of science and technology.

I learned from Descartes as I had learned from Nietzsche the rhetorical benefit of a philosopher telling the story of how he *became* himself. With Nietzsche and Descartes as examples, I was prepared to pay attention when Plato too in his different way put special emphasis on telling the tale of a philosopher *becoming* himself. Plato chose to make available to readers who studied the structures of his dialogues the story of how *Socrates became Socrates*. While omitting the philosophic establishment of modern times, my lectures on Plato and Nietzsche look to the origins of the great tradition of Western philosophy and to its late modern stage as represented by Nietzsche. And with both Plato and Nietzsche I will use their stories of a *philosopher becoming himself* as guidance into their main themes of philosophy and philosophic poetry.

LECTURE 3

Socrates' Philosophic Poetry

Leo Strauss made the difference between the *exoteric* and the *esoteric* in the writings of the philosophers more clear than any previous writer had. Plato was the absolute master of that philosophic art of writing: what you meet first in his dialogues is an exoteric teaching by Socrates that is easily known; careful study of the dialogues, and there are thirty-five of them, leads you to suspect a much less well-known set of conclusions that can be seen only after careful study. Plato's writings make it clear that Socrates is his special teacher. And Plato's writings make many of his readers think of Socrates as *their* special teacher. And for those readers devoted to Socrates, a natural question arises: how did this teacher I so admire *become* himself? Plato has something special to say to such a reader that he makes visible only through a careful study of the dialogues.

Most of Plato's dialogues make it clear *with whom* Socrates is talking and also just *when* and *where* each particular dialogue is taking place. And it is these details of place and time and audience that Plato used to answer the question these readers will have about *how Socrates became Socrates*. And that is the topic shared by both of my Plato lectures.

Plato showed Socrates becoming Socrates in two different respects: *first*, Plato showed how Socrates *the philosopher* came to understand the fundamental truths of being and knowing; he shows the stages of Socrates' development as a thinker about nature and human nature. And *second*, Plato showed how Socrates the philosopher came to understand what it was necessary for a philosopher to *do* in his time and place. Plato shows Socrates' development as a *political philosopher*, as a teacher of a theological-political view, or of what I have called in my titles *philosophic poetry*, for good platonic reasons.

Today I will deal with the second aspect, how Socrates became the *political philosopher* he became. I follow this order for a good platonic reason: Plato leads his reader to Socrates the philosopher through Socrates the political philosopher; he leads to the esoteric or hidden Socrates through the exoteric or evident Socrates.

I begin with Leo Strauss. Strauss began his Plato essay in *The City and Man* by classifying all thirty-five of Plato's dialogues. He treats them as one giant written work of art: each single dialogue belongs within the construct of all the dialogues. Strauss's classification is actually Plato's: it follows a distinction Plato built in to his dialogues. Nine of the thirty-five dialogues are *narrated* or *reported*. That is, we read a text in which some single person speaks or reports the whole dialogue that he witnessed and that the reporter reports to some listener or listeners in the dialogue. And we listen in as the reporter reports. I'll call these the *reported dialogues*. The other twenty-six dialogues are *performed* like a *drama or play*. We read a text presented to us like a play in which each of the characters just speaks his part; the speakers perform their speeches before us. My Plato lectures will leave all twenty-six performed dialogues aside except for occasional reference.

Plato's nine reported dialogues can be further subdivided. In six *Socrates* is the reporter. And in the three others *someone else* is the reporter, in each case a named person.

Today, I will deal with three of the six dialogues reported by Socrates. They are connected to one another initially by another feature that Plato built in to his dialogues, their *dramatic date*; that is, the time or the year in which the dialogue took place, a time in the history of Socrates' life *and* the corresponding time in the history of Athens, Socrates' home. For Plato constructed his dialogues to have a *date*, a discoverable date that often requires his reader to think, *When did this happen?*, and to find the answer that Plato made it possible to find while making the date seem relevant or worth your while to think about.

(A different sort of dating has occupied the Plato scholars: not the time in Socrates' life in which Plato *set* them, but the time in Plato's life in which he supposedly *wrote* them. Dating of this sort, the so-called *composition date*, is always only a scholar's theory and we can do what Strauss did: ignore it entirely in favor of what is not a theory, the dates on which Plato set them.)

On each of the dramatic dates, Socrates was a certain number of years old and *Athens* was at a certain point in its history. Athens was the leading city of Greece in both economic and military power, the center of an empire held together by its ships, merchant ships and war ships. And Athens had become the leading city of the Greek enlightenment, and Plato often showed Socrates in conversation with leading figures of the Greek enlightenment who had come to the imperial city on diplomatic missions or seeking to attract students. Strauss paid close attention to all the details of the dialogues, but he left some very important features of the dramatic dates either not observed or not commented on.

As Strauss said, "The problem inherent in the surface of things, and only in the surface of things, is the heart of things." The surface of things in a Platonic dialogue is a very complex set of details. *Only* a close study of the details can lead the reader to the heart of things, to the most important conclusions. I therefore have to mention a lot of details about the dialogues and only then draw the conclusions. The three dialogues I will deal with today are the *Protagoras*, the *Charmides*, and the *Republic*. Socrates is the reporter in each of these three dialogues. These are the three I spent four hundred pages on in my book, *How Philosophy Became Socratic*, so I have to be selective.

Strauss's first observation about the *Republic* in his *City and Man* essay is this: "While the place of the conversation is made quite clear to us, the time, i.e. the year, is not" (62). But that's *wrong*. Plato made *both* the place and the time, the year, clear in his very first sentence. That sentence runs,

> Down I went yesterday to Piraeus with Glaucon, son of Ariston, to offer prayers to the goddess; and, at the same time, I wanted to observe how they would put on the festival since they were now holding it for the first time.

Plato set the *Republic* on the day the Athenians held the festival of "the goddess" for the first time. A question is built in to this sentence: *which* goddess would have had her festival for the first time during Socrates' lifetime? So there is some *uncertainty* about the date from the first sentence taken by itself. Later in the dialogue, Plato has Thrasymachus refer to the feast of the *Bendideia*; so Plato tells his reader that it is the festival of *Bendis*, a Thracian goddess, a *foreign* god, whose festival was held for the first time in Athens last night in the Piraeus—*last night* because today, Socrates is reporting it in Athens.

So Plato made the date of his *Republic* clear and prominent by putting it in his first sentence and by building in a little uncertainty that he settles later in the dialogue. And *that* day was of course a famous day, a momentous day, on which Athens, pious Athens, did something totally new in the experience of any Athenian alive at that time: *introduce a foreign god* into the gods honored by the city. Pious Athens did not ordinarily invite foreign gods into the gods it honored—and it did so here and now only under great stress.

Plato obviously *wanted* the date of the *Republic* to be known by anyone who gave the question some attention. And every Athenian who did so would know exactly when that was because it was such an important and unprecedented event. What day was that? For us, almost two and half thousand years later, it is hard to learn exactly what day that was. But a student of mine, *Christopher Planeaux*, with ten years of intense single-minded work, made himself a master of all the issues of dramatic dating in Plato's dialogues and assigned each of them their dramatic date. Planeaux settled the date of the *Republic* with some certainty: it was *early June, 429 BCE*.

We can know a lot about that summer because the events that took place then are described by Thucydides, the historian whose book he himself said was "a possession for all time" (1.22). Many of Plato's dialogues, themselves written as possessions for all time, can be assigned their exact dramatic dates because Plato connected them to Thucydides' possession for all time. From Thucydides we can know that 429 is the third year of the great war between Athens and Sparta. And it is the second summer of the great plague that devastated Athens, and Thucydides describes it in horrifying detail. Bendis the Thracian goddess was introduced in early June, 429, partly for war-related strategic reasons, but she was introduced especially because she brought her male consort, a healing god: a hope for healing Athens in the depth of the plague.

So Plato set his *Republic* in a time of extreme Athenian crisis. And the dialogue makes clear that there is another, even more important aspect of that crisis, a *spiritual crisis* that Thucydides describes and that Plato emphasizes, the deepest possible spiritual crisis for a society. So the time, the year of the *Republic* turns out to be very important. And Plato made its importance even greater by the dramatic date he gave to the *Charmides*.

The first sentence of the *Charmides* runs:

> We came on the day before in the evening, from Potidaea, from the army camp, and because I had arrived after some time away, I gladly went around to the places where I usually spend my time.

The first sentence of the *Charmides* also states the day on which it happened, the day after Socrates' return from Potidaea. When was that? With the *Charmides* too, Plato made the exact day a little uncertain in its first sentence because the Athenian army had been at Potidaea for a long time and Socrates, a regular soldier called a *hoplite*, could possibly have returned at some earlier time, even though the army as a whole remained away for some three years. So a little later in the dialogue Socrates says to the person he's reporting it to: "Just before we departed, a battle had occurred at Potidaea which those here had just been learning about." From that comment we learn the exact date of the *Charmides*: it was the day after Socrates returned from the great Athenian defeat at Potidaea when the whole army returned in disarray. Socrates was among the first to return, and those present at the gymnasium where the conversation takes place are eager to hear what happened, who survived and who was killed. And here again, every Athenian who was interested would know *that* date too.

For us, that's two and a half thousand years ago. But Christopher Planeaux determined that date exactly too, partly from Thucydides who reports in detail on the Athenian army's actions in that first campaign of the war and on the great defeat Athens suffered in that battle. As Platonic scholars now recognize: the *Charmides* is set in late May, 429.

And in the *Charmides* Socrates says something remarkable: not only has he been away from Athens for some time, two and a half to three years, but remarkably, he says he comes back *different*, comes back having learned new things from someone he calls "a doctor of Zalmoxis."

So now we see just what Plato did for his interested reader: he set the *Charmides* in late May, 429, and he put that date in the first sentence and made it exact a little later in the dialogue. And he has Socrates say in the *Charmides* that he came back different. And Plato set the *Republic* in early June, 429, a week or two after the *Charmides*, and he put its date in the first sentence and made it exact a little later in the dialogue. And he has Socrates in the *Republic* set out his teaching on justice with all the elaborations that that huge work gives. Strauss shows his reader that there is nothing accidental in Plato's artful dialogues: the close proximity in time that Plato gave to the *Republic* and the *Charmides* forces their interested reader to ask, Why did Plato lead me to wonder why the *Republic* closely follows the *Charmides* in time? How might the *Charmides prepare* me for the *Republic*, the second dialogue of Socrates' return, especially given the arresting fact that Socrates says he returned different?

Once the dramatic dates of the *Charmides* and the *Republic* are linked and the Socrates in these dialogues is seen to be a returning Socrates, returning different, then the question must arise about Socrates *before* his return. Are there dialogues that Plato set *earlier* than 429 BCE? It turns out that the *Protagoras* has a dramatic date that makes it *the first* of the dialogues by dramatic date. Plato made it easy to learn that the *Protagoras* happened before the war, with the great city of Athens at the very height of its power and glory: it is the Athens of Pericles, the Athens of the classical age, when the great marble temples on top of the Acropolis were built. Plato set his *Protagoras* about 434, when the most commanding of all those temples, the Parthenon, was having its decoration completed. Plato set his *Protagoras* before the war broke out, the war that lasted twenty-eight years and left Athens defeated. It is the *chronologically* first of the dialogues, the earliest of them all. (There are other pre-war dialogues, with the *Alcibiades* dialogues being especially relevant to the *Protagoras*, but I must leave them undiscussed here.)

The *Protagoras* is the chronologically first of the dialogues, but there is a noteworthy fact about three other narrated dialogues that Plato set much later in Socrates' life, one at the time of his trial and death, and two after his death. Each of these three dialogues, the *Phaedo*, the *Parmenides*, and the *Symposium*, contains a section, in one of them a very large section, that takes their reader back to a still earlier time in Socrates' life, a time *before* he appears in the *Protagoras* in 434. So each of these three dialogues shows a Socrates *younger* than that Socrates of 434, and what matters most about Plato's three accounts of this younger Socrates is that each of them shows a young Socrates at a *turning point* in his philosophic life. That is something truly special that Plato reserves for his most interested reader: in these three dialogues Plato gives his reader a chance to think about how Socrates became the philosopher he became. These three dialogues show Socrates completing his philosophic education *before* 434, before all the dialogues begin and Socrates mounts the public stage with the *Protagoras* in 434. That will be my topic for my other Plato lecture: *how Socrates became Socrates* (and the topic for my second book on Plato that I am planning to write).

Protagoras

For the rest of today's lecture on the *Protagoras*, the *Charmides*, and the *Republic*, I begin with Socrates in the *Protagoras* in 434. My single, simple question is, Who is the Socrates of the *Protagoras*, a pre-war dialogue? The question matters because in the *Charmides*, the dialogue of Socrates' return from the siege of Potidaea, Socrates says he comes back *different*, having learned something in his absence.

Plato shows that the Socrates of the *Protagoras* had two great aims in the dialogue, and both aims can be seen to belong to philosophy's politics:

One: Socrates arranges a contest in argument with the much older Protagoras, "the wisest man in Greece," the founder of the Greek enlightenment, deservedly famous everywhere in Greece. Socrates, about thirty-six years old, steps forward in order to *restrain* and *redirect* the great Protagoras, who is about sixty-five years old and has never in his life been defeated in argument. One learns from a careful study of the dialogue that Socrates challenges Protagoras because he judges Protagoras to be *too outspoken*; he puts Greek wisdom, Greek philosophy, at risk. Protagoras is *not cautious enough*. Plato himself must be very cautious about this in order to keep philosophy's exoteric practice somewhat veiled, so it is *only* by careful study that one learns that Protagoras too knows the difference between the exoteric and the esoteric. Protagoras *respects* that distinction, but Socrates shows him in a veiled way that his exotericism is much too open and threatens the whole tradition of Greek wisdom. So who is the Socrates of Plato's *Protagoras*? Socrates is a man of the enlightenment who judges that the *founder* of the enlightenment puts the whole enlightenment at risk with his inadequate exotericism. In the *Protagoras* young Socrates warns old and famous Protagoras that he has to be more cautious with the truth.

Two: Plato shows that Socrates' second aim in the *Protagoras* is to attract and win as his own student the young Alcibiades, who is not yet twenty years old. This is also a political aim, because Alcibiades is the *most promising* young Athenian of all those who aspire to political glory and greatness. Thucydides shows Alcibiades to be the great hope of Athens in its war with Sparta. But Alcibiades is attracted by Protagoras, as are other promising Greek young men. Socrates recognizes in Alcibiades a young *political genius* who aspires to rule Greece and is likely do so. And Socrates aims to *win* Alcibiades to himself, to win over the coming political leader of Athens in part to save the Greek enlightenment. Socrates does not aim to persuade Alcibiades to become a philosopher but to maintain in Athens a public spirit friendly to philosophy.

When the *Protagoras*, the most important pre-war dialogue, is understood this way, this *political* way, a question is opened about the *Charmides* and the *Republic*, the two dialogues set just after Socrates returns from a long absence with the army, the two dialogues that Plato set together as the dialogues of a *returning* Socrates who says he comes back *different*, having learned something important while he was away. The question is: *Who is the returning Socrates?* How is he different from the Socrates before the war, the Socrates of the *Protagoras*?

Notice: these questions do not arise from *external* considerations about the dialogues: they arise from problems that Plato built into the surface of the dialogues and that compel their student to raise questions. Only by pursuing the questions inherent in the problems of the surface of the dialogues can the heart of the dialogues be discovered.

Charmides

Plato's *Charmides* answers some of the questions it raises by referring to Homer. All of Plato's contemporary readers knew Homer, the founding poet of Greek civilization revered by all Greeks as the wisest and most authoritative of teachers and memorized by young men inclined to learning. Homer's two epic poems are the *Iliad* on the ten-year war the Greeks fought generations earlier with Troy, and the *Odyssey* on the ten-year return from Troy by Odysseus after the war. Odysseus was the king of Ithaca and the wisest of the Greeks at Troy. Plato quotes or refers to Homer hundreds of times in his dialogues, and his quotations and near-quotations from this founding poet of Greek religion and Greek wisdom are always worth very close attention.

Plato made four references to the *Odyssey* in the *Charmides*, and the four are crucial because in the *Odyssey* wise Homer shows the *return* of the wise king Odysseus after twenty years away. As Seth Benardete argues in *The Bow and the Lyre*, Homer's *Odyssey* shows Odysseus's odyssey to be his gradual learning of the wisdom that is *philosophy* and the wisdom that is *political philosophy*. Benardete makes it possible for us to see that Odysseus, Homer's wise king, is Homer's *philosopher king*. In the *Odyssey* that wise king returns after a long absence to set things right in his kingdom. He returns *masked* as a beggar, returns *hidden* because he has a great task to perform and cannot risk being recognized as himself. In the *Odyssey*, Homer has Odysseus reveal himself in a series of *recognition scenes* to win his necessary allies to accomplish his goal.

With that background we can understand an important feature of the surface of Plato's *Charmides*: its four references to the *Odyssey* are *all* to *recognition scenes*, scenes in which the returning hidden wise king reveals himself to select followers to show them what he must do and to gain their help. Plato put all four references to the *Odyssey* in the proper order, matching the sequence in the *Odyssey*; he made his *Charmides*, his dialogue of Socrates' return from a long absence, match Homer's *Odyssey* in this important way. So *who is* the Socrates returning to Athens in the *Charmides* after his long absence? He is *a new returning Odysseus*, a returning wise king, openly returning but returning hiddenly as a wise man with a political project through which he will rule.

Odysseus's political project in the *Odyssey* is a deed of founding that had two dimensions. The first is a new *political order* that will not be dependent on a rare wise man like himself to rule it: he returns looking to the *succession* of wise rule without wise rulers. The second dimension is to establish a new *teaching on the gods*: Odysseus's purely *political* founding requires a *religious* founding, a wise ruler's alteration of the gods to aid in the succession of wise rule. So the Plato who invites his reader to think of his returning Socrates as Socrates/Odysseus invites him to think of Socrates as returning with a founding deed that is a *theological-political* program.

As Plato arranges things in the *Charmides*, Socrates is introduced to Charmides as a *doctor* who has a drug that might be able to cure Charmides' illness, an illness possibly related to the plague. Forced to play a doctor, Socrates first says he has a certain healing leaf, but for the leaf to be effective certain "*incantations*," magic words or formulas, must be spoken, and the healing *words* gradually replace the leaf in the *Charmides*. Socrates says he learned those incantations while he was away from his teacher, who was a doctor of *Zalmoxis*. Zalmoxis is a god who teaches that to cure the body the soul must also be treated and that the soul can be treated only with incantations which are "beautiful speeches." Socrates adds that the doctors of Zalmoxis "even *immortalize* people"—the doctors of Zalmoxis teach that the soul is immortal.

By bringing in Zalmoxis, Plato refers to *Herodotus*, the Greek historian, without mentioning his name. Plato's reader can learn more about Zalmoxis from Herodotus, who shows that the people who believe in Zalmoxis believe that they are *immortal* and that their god is *the only God*. And Herodotus adds that the people who believe this, the Getae, are *the most courageous and most just* of peoples, the only people to effectively resist the Persian invaders—he thus implies that belief in one God and in the immortal soul made the believers courageous and just, made them virtuous. By referring to Zalmoxis and thereby to Herodotus, Plato tells us more about the Socrates returning to Athens after a long absence. This new Odysseus, this wise king returning to establish a new regime and to bring a new teaching about the gods, returns having learned beautiful healing speeches that teach that there is only one God and that the soul is immortal—the doctor of Zalmoxis taught Socrates the teaching of the *Republic*. By placing his *Charmides* a few weeks before his *Republic* and by having it announce a new teaching it does not elaborate, Plato forces his careful reader to conclude that

Socrates' teaching on the gods and the soul in the *Republic* is the new *political* project of a Socrates returning hiddenly as Socrates/Odysseus.

The *Charmides* is a short dialogue, and after the things I just mentioned it deals mostly with the topic of *moderation*. Socrates discusses moderation with Critias, the most brilliant of his students before he left with the army. The dialogue intimates that Critias had learned from Socrates a view that would eventually turn him into a notorious Athenian criminal, a most immoderate sophist and tyrant in the Athenian civil war. In the *Charmides* Socrates learns that he had corrupted Critias—another powerful reason for altering his teaching. I must omit this important topic, the most prominent topic of the *Charmides*, because it would take us away from my main point here.

I can end that main point about Socrates as a returning Odysseus with this: Plato ends the *Charmides* with Socrates having taught *none of the healing words* he says he brought back, and a reader paying close attention will see that fact about the *Charmides*. But by ending his *Charmides* this way and placing it just before his *Republic* Plato allows that reader and only that reader to draw the conclusion Plato hid just for him: the teaching of the *Republic* is the teaching of a Socrates/Odysseus who returns different from a long absence and aims to found a new political order based on a foreign, non-Homeric teaching about the gods and the soul.

And with that I can turn to the Socrates of the *Republic* and begin to justify my title for today's lecture: *Socrates' Philosophic Poetry*. I can begin to show the way in which Socrates' *philosophic poetry* is what Strauss said it was, *ministerial*, in the service of philosophy and aiding or caring for the sick and wounded.

Republic

The returning Socrates as Odysseus

Plato names Odysseus in the *Republic* only twice, once near the beginning and once at the end. And he *avoids* the name Odysseus elsewhere, speaking instead of "the wisest man at Troy." Socrates speaks the name Odysseus to end the very first argument of the *Republic*, where he also names Homer for the first time. He says: "The just person, it seems, has come to light as a kind of thief, and I'm afraid you learned this from Homer. For he admires Autolycus, Odysseus's grandfather on his mother's side who surpassed all men 'in stealing and in swearing oaths.'"

Autolycus means Wolf Himself and *swearing oaths* means tying your actions to the gods: it is *an act of piety*; Autolycus combines stealing and piety. Autolycus gave Odysseus the name Odysseus: giving his grandson that name is symbolic of this wise grandfather *passing on his wisdom* to his grandson. And Socrates adds: "Justice, it seems, according to you and Homer . . . is a certain art of stealing, for the benefit of friends." Polemarchus, the young man Socrates is talking with, of course did *not* mean that, and if the definition of justice that he offered implies that, then he believes that he had to be *wrong*. But Socrates *did* mean that: the practical wisdom of the wise man is a certain art of stealing in which the pious-looking wise man steals sons away from their fathers by making those sons his own followers, to their great benefit—and that is what Socrates the teacher will do with the young men he speaks to in the *Republic*.

So at the opening of the *Republic* stands this identification of Odysseus as having his grandfather's characteristics. The only other time the *Republic* names Odysseus is at the end of its closing myth, the last lesson of the *Republic*. That famous myth pictures the immortal souls choosing their next life after their long period of reward or punishment in Hades. The souls typically make hasty and foolish choices. But the last soul to make its choice is different:

> And by chance Odysseus's soul had drawn the last lot of all and went to choose; from memory of its former labors it had recovered from love of honor; it went around for a long time looking for the life of a private man who minds his own business; and with effort it found one lying somewhere neglected by others.

The *Republic* ends suggesting that the soul of Odysseus chooses *the life of Socrates*, the life of a private man who minds his own business, the business of philosophy and everything it entails to protect itself and advance itself. Notice: It is the *soul of Odysseus* that makes that choice. It is not *Odysseus* himself but the soul that in a way he got from Autolycus, his grandfather on his mother's side who gave him his name.

So Plato's *Republic* never really names Odysseus himself. Instead, it refers first to one of Odysseus's *forefathers*, a *wise man prior* to Odysseus. And it refers last to Odysseus's *successor, the wise man after* Homer's Odysseus, Socrates himself. Plato in the *Republic* makes the returned Socrates of the *Charmides* the thinker who recognized in himself the soul of Odysseus. Socrates, Plato suggests, carries on and advances the tradition of Greek wisdom that began before wise Odysseus, before Homer, and was passed on after improvements by Homer, and is passed on to Socrates, that "son" of Homer who improves Homeric wisdom and passes it on to his "sons" after him.

"*Improves*" may be the wrong word: what Plato seems to suggest in the *Republic* is that Socrates *adapts or adjusts* Greek wisdom to the new conditions introduced into Greece by the passage of time, one condition in particular being the most important, as we will see. Plato's suggestion seems to be this: a wise man knows *who he is* and he knows *where he is* and he learns what *he must do* because of who he is and where he is.

That's the first of the two things that Plato shows his reader by putting the *Charmides* just before the *Republic* in time. Thinking about that arrangement of the two dialogues, the reader can think of Socrates' innovations or novel teachings in the *Republic* as the work of a wise returning Odysseus.

The returning Socrates as a student of Zalmoxis

In the *Charmides* Socrates says he came back different. To return different is to return different from what Plato had shown Socrates to be before, that is, in his *Protagoras*. The *Charmides* suggests that Socrates came back as a kind of doctor who had learned a curing art while he was away. He came back having learned certain *incantations* or magic words that can cure sick souls, and he learned those curing words from the follower of a foreign god.

Socrates does not speak one word of his healing incantations in the *Charmides*. But a few weeks later, on *the perfect occasion*, Socrates introduces a new teaching into Athens. In the *Republic* the returning Odysseus, Socrates, teaches the incantations he learned while he was away. And the occasion is perfect because while Socrates is introducing *his* teachings from the foreign god Zalmoxis, outside the house in the port of Piraeus, on that very night, the Athenians were themselves importing a foreign god, Bendis.

In the *Charmides* the healing words were supposed to heal Charmides' sickness in the head. And in the *Republic*?

While it takes place in the Athens suffering from the plague, it shows that there is another form of sickness in Athens, a sickness more important and more disastrous than even the plague.

The main conversation of the *Republic*, between Socrates and the two brothers Adeimantus and Glaucon, takes place only after the brothers have made long speeches (Book 2). Those speeches show that these two talented young men have been exposed to the Greek enlightenment and learned the teaching of teachers like Protagoras, teachings that seem to them to destroy the reasons for living a moral life, a life of justice. They are young gentlemen of genuine decency and they want to live decent lives, but they have been seriously shaken by the teaching of Protagoras and others. They *demand* of Socrates that he prove to them that the just life is better than the unjust life.

From their two speeches Plato's reader learns just what the deepest crisis is that grips the Athens to which the new Odysseus returns: it is not only the war and the plague but the greatest possible crisis, a spiritual and moral crisis that I think we can call *the crisis of the death of the gods*, Homer's gods. Adeimantus and Glaucon speak for all decent young Athenians caught up in the war and the plague and exposed to the enlightenment brought by teachers like Protagoras. Protagoras's insufficient exotericism, his failure to hide adequately his own skeptical views, has led the younger generation to mistrust their gods.

So the Socrates who returns different returns to a *different Athens*, an Athens in which the war, the plague, and the enlightenment have made doubt about morality and the gods a crisis of civilized life, a crisis that is the greatest of all emergencies, a crisis similar to what Nietzsche would call *nihilism*.

Reading Plato's *Republic* with Plato's *Charmides* in mind, as Plato invited us to do by setting them a few weeks apart, we learn how the returning Odysseus, Socrates, responds to the spiritual crisis faced in particular by the decent young men who have learned some of the thinking of the all-too-rash wise, the incautious wise like Protagoras.

And here Plato's chronological arrangement of the three dialogues, *Protagoras, Charmides, Republic,* allows us to compare the political philosopher Socrates before the war to the political philosopher Socrates who returned different to a different Athens. By making such a comparison possible Plato allows his devoted reader to see Socrates *becoming* Socrates, becoming in 429, at about age forty, the mature political philosopher that he would remain all his life. His concerns remain what they were in *Protagoras*, the Greek enlightenment and the Athenian young, but his way of dealing with each has changed.

First: With respect to Socrates' aim to moderate the Greek enlightenment, to teach Protagoras and the followers of this founder of the Greek enlightenment to practice a more effective exotericism. In the *Republic* Thrasymachus is the representative teacher of the Greek enlightenment; as a leading figure of the next generation of sophists he is much less restrained or moderate than Protagoras was. He is much more open about expressing the real and radical position of enlightenment teachers, less concerned with giving his teaching an exoteric shelter—although we must remember that in the *Republic* Thrasymachus is speaking in private to a select audience.

Leo Strauss showed beautifully that in the *Republic*, Socrates makes a special effort to win Thrasymachus as his *friend*. At an important point near the middle of the dialogue Socrates even says that he and Thrasymachus have *just become friends without having been enemies before*—although Thrasymachus began, near the beginning of the dialogue, by acting as if they *were* enemies in order to gain an advantage over Socrates with the young men. Socrates' strategic aim in the *Republic* is to persuade Thrasymachus that he can best serve his own advantage by adopting Socrates' strategy for philosophy. Speaking to the young men, his prospective customers and clients, as a friend of Socrates would entail that Thrasymachus *adopt a version* of Socrates' moderate strategy for philosophy.

With respect to the Greek enlightenment then, the Socrates of the *Republic* has learned a new strategy that may succeed with its enlightened teacher, Thrasymachus, as Socrates' pre-war Socrates strategy did not succeed with Protagoras, the founding teacher of the Greek enlightenment.

Second: With respect to Socrates' aim to attract and direct the Athenian young. The *Republic* shows that Socrates has learned a moderate strategy for the public presentation of philosophy that could make him more successful with the young men than he was with Alcibiades. For Socrates learned before the war that he had failed with Alcibiades, as Plato allows us to learn from Alcibiades himself in the *Symposium*. Of course, there is no Alcibiades among the young men with whom Socrates speaks on his return from Potidaea. Alcibiades is an incomparable political genius, one of a kind. Instead, Socrates speaks with Adeimantus and Glaucon, and with Polemarchus and other young men more typical of the talented politically ambitious young men who can be effective leaders in a democratic order like Athens. They are young, spirited gentlemen who aspire to fulfill the role of the gentleman in Athens, a public-spirited political and military role.

For this second way in which Plato showed Socrates

becoming himself with respect to political philosophy, the *Charmides* is crucial because in the *Republic* we hear what the returning Odysseus of the *Charmides* actually returns to *teach*. In the *Republic* we hear the promised healing incantations that are the "beautiful speeches"; we hear what Socrates as a follower of Zalmoxis is prepared to teach. With the preparation Plato gave his reader in the *Charmides* we can understand the meaning of the main teachings of the *Republic*, teachings on *the soul*, on the *knowledge of reality*, and on *the gods*. Socrates' new teachings are all anti-Homeric teachings foreign to the Greek tradition, teachings meant to persuade and cure young men like Adeimantus and Glaucon. I will summarize these three teachings very briefly with what is necessarily a very simplified summary.

First, the returned Socrates teaches a new anti-Homeric view of *the soul*:

Socrates teaches Adeimantus and Glaucon that the soul has a three-part structure and that the *thumotic or spirited part* must be ruled by the *rational part*. The spirited part dominated Greek souls raised on Homer: the young men all desire to be like Achilles, the greatest warrior at Troy. Or even to outdo Achilles, for the Homeric ideal is *competitive*: all the heroes at Troy aim to outdo the others in the virtue of the warrior. Socrates' new teaching on the soul makes the virtue of the spirited part *courage*, which Socrates calls "*political*" courage and places under the rule of the rational part.

Socrates adds a new element to his teaching on the soul with his argument in Book 10: he proves to his young listeners that the soul is *immortal*. This foreign, non-Homeric view of the soul includes Socrates' non-Homeric teaching on *Hades* or the afterlife. Homer treated Hades as the place that all the shades of humans descend to after death; it is a place

Achilles hates. Socrates makes Hades the place of reward or punishment that souls go to after they die, with rewards in Hades for the good and just and punishment in Hades for the bad and unjust. The returned Socrates' teaching on the soul's afterlife is most clearly a teaching that he learned while he was away, from the doctor of Zalmoxis—or, Plato suggests, perhaps from Herodotus, the Greek historian who reports the teachings of Zalmoxis and their salutary or beneficial effects, and who says that the people of Zalmoxis are most courageous and most just.

Second, the returned Socrates brings a new teaching on *knowing and being*.

This is the famous teaching on the *ideas* in the *Republic*. On this topic, Leo Strauss is almost outspoken. He says in his essay on the *Republic* that "no one has ever succeeded in giving a satisfactory or clear account of this doctrine of ideas." Strauss gives a satisfactory and clear account: he shows that the doctrine is an exoteric teaching that can easily persuade non-philosophers who have been raised to believe in glorious gods like Nike and Dike, the gods of victory and justice. Dike, the goddess of justice is a singular, self-standing, immortal being, the glorious cause of every just human act. The *idea* of justice is similar to the goddess; it is the permanent, unchanging, glorious reality in which every just act participates. Part of Socrates' effort to persuade sophist-influenced young Athenians that justice is better than injustice is to persuade them that justice has a permanent, independent reality that can be known by humans. The young men's learned skepticism about Homer's gods leaves them with a concept of what a god is that prepares them for Socrates' teaching on the ideas. Strauss says, that for us, "to begin with," the doctrine of the ideas "is utterly incredible, not to say that it appears to be fantastic." Those famous words by Strauss prepare his demonstration that the doctrine of ideas is *not* to begin with utterly incredible to Glaucon but in fact easily credible because of what he knows a god is from Homer.

Strauss makes it easy for his reader to understand that Socrates' teaching on the eternal, transcendent ideas is a teaching consciously tied to its time, the time of the death of the Homeric gods; it *is exoteric*; it is *philosophic poetry*; it is not part of the Plato nearest to Strauss's heart. (Of course, there is much more to be learned from the ideas about Socrates' genuine insight into human perception and cognition, or sensing and understanding—but that is a different issue entirely, and not one that would be of interest to Glaucon.)

Third, the returned Socrates brings a new teaching on *the gods* that reforms Homer's gods in a moral way.

This is what Strauss chose to place at the center of his account of the *Republic* in *The City and Man* and that I dealt with in my first lecture. Socrates the legislator lays down two new laws for the gods. The first is that they are the cause only of the good. Here Socrates is explicitly anti-Homer: he quotes Homer who says that Zeus metes out both good and bad to human beings. The second is that the gods do not change their shape or lie. This too is a view of the gods contrary to Homer, and Strauss stresses that Socrates must argue Adeimantus out of the view he inherited from Homer that of course the gods lie. I think it is proper to say that Socrates teaches Adeimantus the lie, the noble lie, that the gods do not lie. It is proper to say that because of *what a god is* in Socrates' view—and with that we touch an issue on which Strauss was very careful but on which he nevertheless made himself clear: he indicated that in Plato's view as in Nietzsche's view gods philosophize or the gods are the philosophers. I will deal with this further in later lectures.

A crucial part of making the gods more moral than Homer had made them is what Socrates adds in Book 10: he makes the gods ultimately responsible for punishing or rewarding the soul after death in Hades.

Socrates teaches an additional new thing about the gods: through his teaching on the ideas and the idea of ideas, the idea of the good, Socrates moves toward the *monotheism* of Zalmoxis. Plato was certainly read that way by the monotheists who were Christians, like Saint Augustine. And this openness to monotheism is an important part of what Nietzsche and other modern philosophers before him regarded as the disastrous consequence of Plato's teaching: it opened the way in the West for the successful introduction of Christianity. I'll say more about this great event too in later lectures.

That is a summary of the new teaching that the returning Socrates brought back from Potidaea. His new teaching is his new *philosophic poetry*, his *ministerial poetry*, as Strauss calls it, his poetry to serve philosophy while ministering to the spiritual needs of the young men like Adeimantus and Glaucon. And this new teaching introduced by Socrates in the summer of 429 is the teaching that remains his mature political philosophy to the end. And Plato means *to the very end*, to 399, because Plato has Socrates repeat in his *Phaedo*, on his last day and with the last argument of his life, the teaching on the ideas that he introduced in 429, thirty years earlier, and he has Socrates tell new stories that teach lessons on the immortal soul and on the gods that are similar to the stories he first told in 429 when he returned from Potidaea.

So paying attention to what Strauss said was not given in the *Republic*, its time, its year, allows us to learn a great deal that helps us understand the *Republic*. Learning that the returning Socrates of the *Charmides* and the *Republic* is returning in the late spring and early summer of 429 allows us to reflect on the sublime setting, the poetically beautiful and fitting setting that Plato gave to "the most famous political *work* of all times." On the very day on which numberless Athenians streamed back up to Athens to report on the all-night spectacle of the introduction of the new goddess, Socrates came back up to Athens to report on what he introduced privately on the same night in the same place and now introduces to whoever wants to hear it in Athens, for Socrates reports the whole *Republic* in Athens to an unidentified audience, to anyone and everyone.

The Athenian introduction of Bendis failed to do anything to change the ultimate fate of Athens. Socrates' introduction of his new teachings succeeded in changing the fate of philosophy in Athens and, ultimately, in changing the fate of Western civilization. Socrates is what Nietzsche says he was, "the one vortex and turning point of so-called world history."

I want to end this lecture by discussing Plato and Homer and Nietzsche.

The Socrates who returned from Potidaea brought anti-Homer teachings. In Book 10 of the *Republic* Socrates makes his criticism of Homer more explicit and more complete. His criticism is meant to break the hold that Homer had on the minds of the young; his criticism helps Socrates replace Homer's teaching and put his own new teaching in place. In a dramatic way, by breaking the power of Homer's influence, Socrates *kills off* Homer and rises to replace him.

But Socrates also honors Homer. As the returning Odysseus, Socrates learned from Homer what Odysseus had to do to be successful. And one of the things that Socrates learned from Homer gave Socrates a kind of permission to kill Homer by supplanting Homer or taking Homer's place as the ultimate authority. In his *Odyssey* Homer emphasizes that the returning Odysseus must kill all one hundred and eight suitors of his wife, Penelope. The suitors compete to marry Odysseus's wife because her husband the king has been gone for twenty years and can reasonably be presumed dead. The suitor who is successful in his suit would marry Odysseus's supposed widow and become king of Ithaca himself. The one hundred and eight suitors represents the old order that will continue in the old way with Odysseus gone and a new rightful king in his place.

The returning Odysseus is Odysseus the king, but Odysseus returns as the *wise* king who knows that he must establish a new order politically and religiously. Politically that means establishing a new order to be ruled by his son, Telemachus, a fine young man but of course not that great rarity that his father is, a wise ruler. Wise Odysseus must see to the succession by establishing a more democratic order to be ruled by Telemachus and his associates like Eumaeus, the loyal pig farmer. But for that new order to succeed all one hundred and eight suitors must die—the new order can be well established only if the old order is wiped out. So of course all the suitors must die.

But right establishment of the new requires that the suitors must not only die: they must seem to *deserve it*, they must be judged wicked, memory of them must be memory of their wickedness. So Homer paints them wicked. Homer makes the memory of them the memory of the wicked suitors that righteous Odysseus brought to justice with the help of Athena herself. Homer does what Machiavelli, more than two thousand years later, explicitly says must be done.

And Socrates? Socrates knows from Homer that he can establish the new order only by killing off the old order. Socrates learns from Homer that he must kill Homer. And Socrates knows from Homer that he must make Homer seem to deserve it. So Socrates teaches that Homer deserves to die, to be supplanted as the ultimate authority, because Homer made Zeus responsible for human evil and Homer was ignorant of the ideas and Homer was ignorant of the soul's immortal destiny. Socrates exoterically and actually killed off Homer, replacing Homer as the ultimate authority and replacing Homer's teaching with his own teaching. But esoterically Socrates honors Homer as his own teacher, as the now passing authority who must give way to his successor, as Autolycus gave way to Odysseus.

And Homer expected to be killed off, he *taught* that he must be killed off by the coming wise man, whoever he was, whenever he came, whatever he brought. That coming wise man learned from Homer that all one hundred and eight suitors must die, that Homer well knew that he must die for the necessary new wise teaching to take root.

Times change, gods die, and politic wisdom must change with the times by teaching new gods.

And for me, there is no better way to begin Nietzsche than that: Nietzsche made every effort to *kill off Plato*, the philosopher who had "the greatest strength any philosopher has so far had at his disposal" (BGE 191). But Nietzsche kills off Plato with Plato's permission, he kills the Plato who killed Homer with Homer's permission, he kills the exoteric Plato whose teaching ultimately led to a cultural disaster.

But Nietzsche *honors* Plato as Plato honored Homer. Plato remains what he was, "the most beautiful growth of antiquity" (BGE Preface), and the most beautiful growth of antiquity is immortal, living on forever in the underworld of the wise as the wise man he esoterically was. But historically there is no going backward, antiquity itself must be supplanted by the late modern as it was first supplanted by the modern. Plato must be supplanted by Nietzsche.

LECTURE 4

Socrates Becomes Socrates

My first Plato lecture dealt with the dialogues that I treated in my published Plato book. Today's Plato lecture is on the Plato book that I have not yet written but that I want to write next, after I finish my new Nietzsche book.

Today's Plato lecture is also on three dialogues, the three narrated or reported dialogues that Plato made unique by making them the only dialogues that are reported by someone other than Socrates, the *Phaedo* reported by Phaedo, the *Parmenides* reported by Cephalus, and the *Symposium* reported by Apollodoros. This lecture too makes use of the dramatic dates that Plato gave his dialogues, the dates on which Plato set the conversations. And these three dialogues have another feature that makes them unique: within each of these dialogues, after the dialogue has started, Plato takes the reader back to an earlier time in Socrates' life, and each of those times comes to light as very significant because in each of them Socrates is at a different stage of his philosophic life and in each of them he learns something crucial for his advancement in philosophic understanding.

If you as a reader think about those three events, think about each in relation to the others, you can very easily put them in the right order, and you have to think that Plato *intended* you to do this work. Plato scattered these three events on purpose, putting them in three different dialogues to which he gave the formal similarity that they are the only ones reported by someone else. Plato's intentional complication has the effect of really getting your attention. It makes you think, there must be more to this, more to learn. Plato must be trying to *teach* me something.

The order that Plato invites you to see is a sequence in time that is a logical sequence in which the *Phaedo* comes first, then the *Parmenides*, and finally the *Symposium*. That logical sequence is Socrates' progress in thought. It begins with Socrates' earliest beginnings as a philosopher in the *Phaedo*, including a step he made wholly on his own, a new step in Greek philosophy. Then comes the step in the *Parmenides*: Parmenides, great Parmenides, shows Socrates that that new view of his is logically inadequate, no, logically impossible, and even if it was possible, we could never know that it was. Learning *that* about his proud invention, Socrates is led to the ultimate step, the point of deepest insight that a philosopher can attain, and he learns that in the *Symposium*.

With these three linked dialogues, linked *formally* as the only dialogues reported by someone other than Socrates, linked *logically* by Socrates' movement from his earliest stages through to his ultimate insight, Plato teaches you, you who are really interested, really working at it, how *Socrates became Socrates*, how the philosopher who is Plato's model, the philosopher Nietzsche said is "the one vortex and turning point of so-called world history," how *that* philosopher became himself. Another way of saying this is that Plato's calculated presentation of the exoteric Socrates is intended to lead his most interested reader to the esoteric Socrates.

There is something else that Plato intentionally built in to this arrangement of three dialogues. Once you see the proper sequence of Socrates' learning and put the steps in the chronological order that Plato intended, you also see that Plato made it possible to date those steps in the life of Socrates against the background of the life of Athens. One important fact about the actual dates that Plato makes it easy to discover is that they all fall before the *Protagoras*. That is, Plato shows that Socrates' private development as a philosopher was in a sense complete before Plato had Socrates first mount the stage as a public teacher in the *Protagoras*.

It is important to see that these details are not some *theory* about the dialogues; they do not *bring* to the text some fixed set of ideas about texts; they are instead features that Plato built into these dialogues without calling undue attention to them. Their presence in the text can be explained only as Plato's intention; he put them in the surface of the text to be noticed by readers who pay close attention and who read with the aim of learning what Plato had to teach and who have already seen that Plato is a master of artful writing who teaches in the way Socrates taught, that is, without saying everything.

Leo Strauss noticed the chronological arrangement of the three dialogues that show Socrates becoming a philosopher. So did Seth Benardete, who called them the "three stages in Socrates' philosophic education." But neither Strauss nor Benardete worked out those stages by linking in detail the three events that Plato arranged. That's what I want to do here and do in much more detail in my next book on Plato.

There is one last complication I have to mention: Plato gave another account of a younger Socrates in his *Apology of Socrates*. There, in his defense speech, Socrates made his famous statement that *the god at Delphi* told his friend Chaerephon that no one was wiser than Socrates. Socrates reports that when he heard what the god said, he *turned* to the way in which he has practiced philosophy ever since. Socrates tells this story to the "*men of Athens*," to all his fellow citizens present at his trial. In his only public speech to all of Athens, his defense speech or his speech of self-explanation, Socrates tells all his fellow citizens a story of how he became himself.

Socrates' speech to the public must be interpreted as a *politic* speech. Socrates says to all his fellow citizens: think of me this way, think that what I do as a philosopher I do in obedience to the god. That is, Socrates tells the men of Athens, I do what I do in obedience to the highest authority that all of you know, the god at Delphi. Socrates' public account of himself is a *mythically* true account of how he became himself: he became himself in obedience to the highest authority. But how is *highest authority* to be understood? Socrates knows that authority to be *reason*, his fellow citizens know that authority to be *the god at Delphi*. The account of Socrates becoming Socrates that Plato spread across three different dialogues, *Phaedo*, *Parmenides*, and *Symposium*, for *you* to discover, is the *non-mythic* account of how Socrates became himself, the account of what his reasoning led him to discover, the account *you* will very much want to learn and will work to learn. That account is the esoteric presentation of the exoteric story Socrates told of his becoming, told everyone, in the *Apology*.

Given these two different accounts in the dialogues, we could ask, *When* did that Delphi event with the god, *that* turn in Socrates' life, occur in the life-sequence of events that Plato made it possible to discover from the dialogues as a whole? That seems to me to be the wrong question for a mythic story. It misunderstands a mythic account by treating it as an historical account. The historic account Plato scattered in the three unique dialogues.

With that preparation, we can begin the substance of what I want to say today. I will follow the logical development that the three dialogues, the *Phaedo, Parmenides,* and *Symposium*, show Socrates following in becoming himself.

Phaedo

The *Phaedo* is reported by Phaedo, who was one of the frequent visitors to Socrates in his prison cell and who was present on the last day when Socrates talked with his friends and then drank the poison and died. Phaedo reports his story of Socrates' last day to a group of *Pythagoreans* in Phlia, a city in the Peloponnese far from Athens. The Pythagoreans were a school of Greek philosophers whose teaching had some influence on Socrates. And the Pythagoreans at Phlia were interested in Socrates. So Plato could perhaps be suggesting that the already existing Pythagorean schools could be one possible means of carrying forward the memory of Socrates and what he taught.

Phaedo reports for the Pythagoreans what happened on Socrates' last day and what Socrates said on his last day. On the day he was to die by drinking the poison when the sun went down, most of what Socrates said was about what happened to the soul at death, and Pythagoreans already believed that the soul was immortal. Two young Pythagoreans had also been regular visitors to Socrates' cell, but these two young men had doubts; they wondered if what they had been taught about their immortal souls was really *true*. So most of the conversation that day was Socrates presenting arguments to these two young Pythagorean doubters in order to persuade them by arguments that their souls were in fact immortal.

Phaedo's report leads finally to one last reason to doubt, which is stated by *Kebes*, one of the young men present. Socrates pauses before he answers. He pauses before his final argument that day, the argument he knows will be *the last argument of his life* because the sun is sinking and he has to drink the poison at sundown. He pauses, he says, because the objection Kebes raised requires that he consider "the cause concerning generation and destruction as a whole." Kebes' question concerns the comprehensive topic of philosophy, the *cause* at work in the whole of nature, the whole of becoming. To deal with that great topic of the cause of coming into being and passing out of being, Socrates offers to "go through my own experiences about them." And then Socrates goes back to the very first philosophical reflections of his life.

So Plato has arranged *something remarkable*: before the *last argument of his life*, Socrates goes back to his *first philosophic experiences* in order to tell the story of his becoming a philosopher from its very beginning.

Socrates says that "as a young man I was wondrously desirous of that wisdom they call 'inquiry into nature.'" The youngest Socrates we ever see in Plato was a young man with a passionate desire to understand nature as a whole, a young man who was what the Western tradition of philosophy came to call a "pre-Socratic philosopher." As Socrates reports it on his last day, he came to see problems in the way the early Greek philosophers of nature explained cause in terms of natural causes at work in nature. While investigating those problems of cause he found no way out of the problems until he heard about a philosopher who explained change in nature as caused by Mind as the ordering cause. According to this explanation of cause, everything in nature is what it is because it was *for the best* that it be that way, as judged by mind. All events of coming into being and passing out of being could be explained *teleologically*: everything that happened happened because of the *goal* or *end* intended for it by ruling Mind. When Strauss deals with this view in *Xenophon's Socratic Discourse*, he calls it Socrates' *teleotheology*, a word invented by Strauss to express the view that the gods rule the world by causing each event to be directed toward the best end.

But Socrates reports in Plato's *Phaedo* that when he read the books of this teacher of teleology, Anaxagoras, he found that the teacher himself did not use that form of explanation, he did not show how this thing or that thing is what it is because it is best that it be that way. Instead, even Anaxagoras looked to *natural causes* and not to Mind. (This may be an indication of Anaxagoras's own use of exoteric and salutary teaching to cover his own esoteric naturalism.)

Socrates goes on to say on his death day that natural causes alone cannot explain human things, such as what caused him to be sitting in prison waiting to drink the poison. The *true causes* of that fact cannot be explained by the actions of his "bones and sinews" but have to be explained by human opinion, what human beings judge is for the best, what Athenians judge is best for them, that Socrates die, and what Socrates judges is best for him—that he drink the poison that Athenians say he deserves. So natural causes are not enough to explain all events, in particular human events; and an all-governing Mind seems also not to be an adequate explanation. What *is* the cause of generation and destruction as a whole?

And here, before the last argument of his life, Socrates says that very early in his life he devised his *own way*, and he asks the young Pythagorean, Kebes: ". . . do you want me to make a display . . . of the way by which I've busied myself with the second sailing in search of the cause?" A "second sailing" is a metaphor from the Greek experience with ships: when the wind does not blow and fill the sails, the traveler has to use another means, he has to use *the oars*, he has *to row*. Socrates explains his philosophical "second sailing" as a turn away from the things to be explained and a turn toward the speeches or accounts that human beings use to talk and think about the things: perhaps in the speeches, in the *logoi*, he will find the proper cause for the things. In Socrates' words for this turn to the speeches he says this: "I'm going to try to show you the form (*eidos*, idea) of the cause with which I've busied myself." And that, he says, was the way he began with the *ideas* or *forms* that he has been talking about ever since.

The particular ideas he talks about in the *Phaedo* are the idea of the *Beautiful*, the idea of the *Good*, the idea of *Bigness*. And the basic thought is that every beautiful thing is beautiful because it *participates* in the Beautiful itself—the Beautiful, the idea of the beautiful, never changes but each beautiful thing does: it becomes beautiful and then ceases to be beautiful; it comes to participate in the beautiful and then ceases to participate in the beautiful. It's not important now to understand more of Socrates' "theory of ideas"—as Strauss says, "for us, to begin with it is utterly incredible, not to say that it appears to be fantastic." All that matters for us is that *this* is what Socrates, the young philosopher passionate about the explanation of cause in the events in nature, *turned to* when he was dissatisfied with what his predecessors in Greek philosophy had said about the cause of all generation and destruction as a whole.

And he says on his last day that he is still using this way of talking about the ideas to explain cause. And in the last argument of his life that he now begins, Socrates uses the ideas to prove that the soul is immortal. And young Kebes finds it completely persuasive; now he knows by argument that his soul is immortal. Now he can let Socrates die because Socrates cured his doubt—one more reason to owe a cock to Asclepius for a healing.

Socrates was about seventy years old when he made this last argument of his life and then drank the poison. How old was Socrates when he made that turn to the ideas that he has been talking about ever since? How old was he when he made these first steps in his philosophic life, starting with the Greek philosophers of nature and his turn to the ideas? He does not say, but Plato lets his reader know in the *Parmenides*. So we can now look at the *Parmenides* in order to get clearer about this first stage of Socrates becoming Socrates.

Parmenides

Plato set the conversation reported in the *Parmenides* at a famous moment in the philosophic history of Athens, a moment that all Athenians with an interest in intellectual things would know: it was the famous visit of the great philosophers *Parmenides* and *Zeno* to Athens. That visit occurred in 450 BCE at an Athenian festival, the great Panathenaia that Plato refers to. The Socrates who speaks to Parmenides and Zeno is a "very young" man, says a speaker in the *Parmenides*, but he has already developed his view of the ideas, because he uses the ideas to challenge the old philosopher Parmenides and his younger follower, Zeno, challenge them and win a great victory for himself.

That means that Socrates' turn to the ideas that he reports in the *Phaedo* came earlier than this 450 conversation. In 450 Socrates was about *nineteen years old*. So Socrates' passionate engagement with natural philosophy, and then his insights into the problems with natural cause, and then his enthusiasm for teleology and his recognition of *its* limits as an explanation of cause, and finally even his *turn* to the speeches and to the *ideas* as cause all came before or when he was about nineteen. So Plato shows something remarkable about Socrates: he was a *philosophic prodigy*, a *young genius in philosophy* who by age nineteen had thought through the whole history of Greek philosophy before him and arrived at his own novel solution to the problem of cause, his view of the ideas.

The setting of the *Parmenides*

The setting that Plato gave his *Parmenides* tells us why there still exists a record of the conversation that the nineteen-year-old Socrates had with two mature, famous philosophers, sixty-five-year-old Parmenides and his forty-year-old disciple, Zeno. It is a complicated but very important setting for anyone who is interested in how Socrates became Socrates.

The narrator or reporter of the *Parmenides* is a man named *Cephalus*; he is one of the "men of Clazomenae," a Greek city in Asia Minor, who sailed across the Aegean sea to Athens to find out if *the one person* who *might have memory* of that conversation is still able to remember what was said about sixty years ago—the "frame" of the *Parmenides* having been set by Plato about 394 BCE (as the fixing of the dramatic dates by Christopher Planeaux shows). The men of Clazomenae had heard that that person had been taught when he was young to memorize everything that was said that day by a man who had actually been present in 450 and heard it all and memorized it himself. It is far too late to ask Socrates or any other participant about it; they are all dead.

When the men of Clazomenae arrive in Athens, Plato has them run into Adeimantus and Glaucon in the marketplace, the two main characters from the *Republic*, and it is their half-brother, Antiphon, that they are looking for. Together, they all go to Antiphon to learn if he can still remember the speeches he had memorized years ago. Antiphon does still remember what he memorized, but he does not want to go through the hard work of saying it all again. He has lost all interest in it, but the men of Clazomenae persuade him to work at recalling it all anyway.

The 450 B.C.E. Conversation

In the first stages of the conversation that Antiphon reports to the men of Clazomenae, the young Socrates presents his view of the ideas as something he himself devised; and he presents it in the way a nineteen-year-old philosophic innovator would present it: he is proud, competitive, victory-loving; he is eager to prove that these two famous philosophers are *wrong* and that he, only he, solved their great problem, the problem of cause. It's all a contest, and the nineteen-year-old just knows that he will be the victor.

The man who was present in 450, Pythodorus, was sure that Parmenides and Zeno would be *angry* at being treated that way. But no, they *admired* Socrates for what he said. That is, they saw in the young Socrates a man of their own kind, a great rarity of the kind a philosopher always seeks.

After Socrates made his proud speech refuting them, Parmenides raised a first logical difficulty with Socrates' view of transcendent, fixed ideas. Socrates has no answer to that difficulty so Parmenides says to him:

> Well, you're still young, Socrates, and philosophy has not yet taken hold of you as it will, in my opinion . . . As for now, you still look to the opinions of men, because of your age.

Parmenides thus suggests to the young thinker, Socrates, that there is way too much love of victory driving him, the "opinions of men" still matter far too much to him, but Parmenides believes there is great promise in Socrates.

Parmenides then raises deeper and even more serious arguments against the possibility of the view that Socrates thought would bring him victory. Socrates has no argument that can defend transcendent ideas against Parmenides' arguments. At the end of these unanswerable arguments Parmenides says to Socrates:

> Only a *naturally gifted man* could learn that there is a certain kind and beinghood in itself for each thing; and only a *still more wondrous person* will discover all these things and be able to teach someone else to be able to judge them clearly and sufficiently for himself.

Could *Socrates* be that "naturally gifted man" who can learn that there is a certain kind and being in itself for each thing? Parmenides is challenging young Socrates. It seems that Socrates has made the fundamental step of philosophy and learned for himself that things have *natures*, that each thing belongs to a *kind*, a natural kind: that is what the "idea" of a thing means. But in the competitive battle that this conversation is, the older philosopher challenges young Socrates even further: could *you* be that "still more wondrous person" who will be able to discover all these things and also "be able to teach someone else to be able to judge them clearly and sufficiently for himself"?

Fine old Parmenides brings his challenge to an end by telling the young Socrates why it is necessary for him to push forward in thinking about the ideas and not take his defeat as a refutation of the very notion of the ideas:

> "And yet," said Parmenides, "if someone, in turn, Socrates, after focusing on all these problems and others still, shall *deny* that there are ideas of the beings and will not distinguish a certain idea of each single thing, wherever he turns he'll understand nothing, since he does not allow that there is an ever-same idea for each of the beings. And so he will entirely destroy the power of dialogue or dialectics. But you seem to me only too aware of this."

The very possibility of understanding is at stake in the ideas. If things are to be understood at all, then each thing must have its idea, must be an instance of its own kind. It must have a nature. And furthermore, that nature must in some sense be knowable. For *philosophy* to be possible at all, things must have natures or be of a kind, and these kinds must in some sense be knowable. Do you have it in you, Socrates, to move beyond your refuted view of the ideas? Are you one of *that* kind, *our* kind, Zeno and me? Does your natural genius extend so far that you will be able to discover and to show others the grounds of the possibility of philosophy? Socrates of course knows that Parmenides' arguments have proven that his view of the ideas is rationally indefensible. It is *wrong*. But will he be able to meet Parmenides' challenge? Is he of the same kind as the great Parmenides, whom he thought he could refute with his now refuted view?

What a story *that* is. Cephalus had identified the men of Clazomenae as "quite the philosophers." And hearing that story, they must have rejoiced at their decision to sail across the sea in the mere hope of hearing a story about a young Socrates conversing with Zeno and Parmenides.

The implications of the setting and the conversation

Pythodorus was there in 450 and heard everything. It was at his house that Parmenides and Zeno were staying while they were in Athens. *He*, the host of these great philosophers, knew the importance of what he was hearing with the young Socrates and he memorized it. Then, much later, concerned that what he had heard and memorized be preserved, he passed on what he had memorized to his young friend, Antiphon, and helped *him* to memorize it. But Antiphon lost interest in it; he failed to see why it had to be passed on, and he does not want to go to all the trouble of trying to remember it. The story would have died with him except for the men of Clazomenae.

And what about Adeimantus and Glaucon, the young men taught by Socrates in the *Republic* in 429, forty years ago now?—394 being the time in which Plato set the *Parmenides*. Plato has made it clear that Adeimantus and Glaucon had no real interest in this story of the young Socrates: in all those years they never bothered to ask their brother to tell them the story of the young Socrates. For all *they* cared, the story would have died with their brother.

And that seems to me perfectly right and instructive: they heard what Socrates had to teach them as young men after Socrates himself had learned his proper poetry, his proper exoteric teaching. And that was enough for them. With that they learned all the lessons of the *Republic*, all the main lessons of Socrates' public teaching, and they were fully satisfied with that. For them, Socrates is the teacher of the view that they are now fully content to *believe* as the grounds of their lives of justice and decency. Socrates taught them how to get over the doubts caused by the Greek enlightenment and he taught them the nature of their souls, and the fixed permanence of the ideas, and of moral gods who will reward their justice in Hades.

But the men of Clazomenae? They are different from Antiphon and Adeimantus and Glaucon in the essential way: they have to know what the young Socrates said to or learned from the great Parmenides and Zeno. They have already learned enough about Socrates to know that they must hear this story of his early thinking. In the language I'm using here, they want to learn how Socrates *became* Socrates, how Socrates became the philosopher that they so admire, admire so much that they are willing to cross the sea on the basis of a mere rumor that that story of the young Socrates might still be heard.

So this is what Plato seems to be saying by setting up the *Parmenides* this way: The only ones who can really care about hearing this important event in the young Socrates' life are nameless latecomers from abroad, some few willing to sail across the sea in the mere hope of learning what a young Socrates and an old Parmenides said to one another. Plato seems to be saying that what he, Plato, preserves in this dialogue is only for the passionately interested few, nameless future travelers from afar, potential philosophers willing to expend a lot of time and effort to learn what even close associates of Socrates do not need to know.

It seems that this is how Plato thinks the tradition of philosophy works, how Socratic philosophy will be passed down: the essential esoteric Socrates is embedded in the preserved conversations of the exoteric Socrates. Those conversations can continue to train the Adeimantuses and

Glaucons in the edifying, moral teaching with which philosophy will be identified and which they will believe. But there will be those few, those who correspond to the nameless men of Clazomenae in being driven to inquire further, driven to investigate the Socratic speeches in order to understand what is esoterically sheltered in them: they will not simply believe what Socrates tells them, they will work to understand what Socrates is also implying, and they will test that and judge that for themselves.

The men of Clazomenae learn what Socrates learned at nineteen. They learn that the doctrine of transcendent fixed ideas, the doctrine Adeimantus and Glaucon trust, is impossible. That's their reward for their needing to know what old Parmenides said to young Socrates. And after learning that, they know that their travels must continue, they must follow Socrates' learning further. To what? We can assume that Plato left that question open in order to have it be pursued in the way that he himself arranged.

For Plato, the author of all these stories, *records* this great event in Socrates' past, this turning point in the process of Socrates becoming Socrates, the event that forced Socrates to abandon transcendent ideas as an adequate understanding of cause. And Plato shows a lot more by the chronological sequence he gave these two dialogues. Clearly, Plato's *Parmenides* shows the Socrates who had already made the first step in philosophy that Plato showed in the *Phaedo*. The *Parmenides* shows the second step in the philosophic education of Socrates. But by *linking* the *Phaedo* and the *Parmenides* this way, Plato forces his reader to confront a very big problem: On the last day of his life, at age seventy, in the last argument of his life, Socrates teaches young Pythagoreans the very view of the ideas that he himself, fifty years earlier, learned from Parmenides was rationally indefensible.

And Socrates says on his last day that this is what he always brings in, the ideas as cause. Of course Socrates never forgot what Parmenides did with this view of the ideas. So why is he still teaching, on the last day of his life, and why has he always been teaching, the view that he learned was rationally indefensible when he was nineteen?

The *Phaedo* itself indicates why without saying why: in the *Phaedo* Socrates repeatedly calls his last argument using the ideas *the safe view*, the view his young audience can *trust*; it is the view he encourages them even *to shout* whenever anyone argues for a contrary view. And they do trust it; they do believe it; and we can imagine them shouting it. Believing the ideas this way, they will not be victims of the doubts and fears that they express in the *Phaedo*. And that's enough for them, just as the *Republic* was enough for Adeimantus and Glaucon. They do not go on to question Socrates' last argument, as Socrates himself suggests that even the last argument of his life, the argument based on the ideas, might be questioned—and in fact is questioned, by someone, "I don't remember who," Phaedo says. By not questioning the argument from the ideas, by just believing it, the two young men prove one thing: they are not of Socrates' kind. They would never sail across the sea in hopes of hearing a story of Socrates' origins.

The *Phaedo* and the account of the young Socrates in *Parmenides* are separated by fifty years. By linking the last day of Socrates' life to the day he learned that the ideas are not an adequate explanation of cause, Plato shows that that view of the ideas in the *Republic* and the *Phaedo* belongs to political philosophy as a safe view that makes philosophy publicly defensible as morally trustworthy. It is a part of philosophic poetry, part of what Strauss called ministerial poetry. But we are still left with the serious philosophical problem that

Socrates already had at age nineteen, the problem of understanding nature, understanding cause. And with that as the problem we can move directly to the third and last stage of Socrates' philosophic education in the *Symposium*.

Symposium

Leo Strauss gave two reasons for holding that the *Symposium* is Plato's most important dialogue: it is the only dialogue whose topic is *praise of a god*, Eros or Love. And it is the only dialogue named for its occasion, the event at which it happened: a *drinking party* at which wine loosens tongues and things are said that might otherwise not be said. From these two visible points, Strauss moves to a hidden feature of the *Symposium* suggested by its dramatic dates: this dialogue *profanes the mysteries*, it tells what it is a crime to tell, a secret about the gods and what they know.

Important guidance to the *Symposium* is also supplied by Seth Benardete. What I have to say about the *Symposium* makes use of both Strauss and Benardete, especially Benardete.

In the *Phaedo*, Phaedo tells the story of Socrates' last day at which he was present; but within the story he tells, Socrates himself reports his earliest beginning in the philosophic life. In the *Parmenides*, two memorized recollections take the reader back to the actual conversation in which the nineteen-year-old Socrates speaks. And again in the *Symposium*, two memorized recollections take the reader back to the actual conversation reported, and there it is again Socrates who tells the story of this last stage of his becoming himself, a story he wants to tell of his much younger self—and he knows a devoted follower is listening to everything because he invited that follower to the party.

The *Symposium* has a complicated chronology. It opens at a time when two different groups of Athenians have a great interest in hearing about a drinking party at Agathon's house at which Socrates and Alcibiades and others made speeches about Eros. Christopher Planeaux shows that that frame for the dialogue is set in 399, just before the trial of Socrates: that's the reason for all that interest in Socrates and Alcibiades.

Why is 399 significant?

First, it is significant because it is the time of Socrates' trial. Part of the charge against him originated in the suspicion that he corrupted Alcibiades—and many Athenians regarded Alcibiades as a great criminal partly or even mostly because he was suspected of profaning the mysteries in 416. The *Symposium* demonstrates that Socrates is innocent of the charge that he corrupted Alcibiades; the two supplied audiences for the reporting of the *Symposium* can therefore judge Socrates innocent of that charge. Another trial in Athens in 399, the trial of Andokides, likely just before Socrates' trial, showed that the 416 crimes were a pressing, much talked about issue because Andokides was tried for being involved. This trial, like Socrates' trial, was an event in the purification of the city of Athens after the war with Sparta ended in 404 and after the civil war against the thirty Tyrants who were led in part by *Critias*, the other great Athenian who was thought to have been corrupted by Socrates. 399 was a time of fervent religious purification to which Socrates fell victim.

There's a second reason that 399 is important. In his defense speech at his trial, Socrates told the story that became famous: the god at Delphi said that no one was wiser than he was, and that made him turn to what became his customary practice in service to the god, testing what the god said. This story, as I said, we can regard as mythically true. But in the *Symposium*, also set in 399 when Socrates told that story about himself, we hear the deeper truth about how Socrates became himself—in the *Symposium* we hear Socrates tell the genuine origin story of his wisdom.

The 399 reporter is Apollodoros, who says that he got the story from Aristodemos, who was there because Socrates invited him. The party was held the second night after Agathon, the host, won the tragedy contest. As the writer of a prize-winning tragedy, Agathon was famous; all Athenians would know that his victory occurred in 416.

Why is 416 significant?

Everyone knows that the shocking crime of profaning the mysteries happened in 416, the crime of revealing the secret core of Athenian religion. Alcibiades was widely thought to be guilty of that crime, of having ridiculed and exposed the most sacred secrets. Studying the *Symposium* with that crime of revealing secrets in mind leads the reader to see what Strauss emphasizes: a profaning of different mysteries, the mysteries of what a philosopher is and what a philosopher can know. Socrates' speech at the drinking party, that setting for loosened tongues, opens for inspection the most hidden truths about philosophy that Plato will ever reveal, an unveiling of the mystery of Socrates' being as a philosopher that is at the same time an unveiling of the mystery of being itself. The crime of profaning the mysteries of Athenian religion violates Athenian law. But the mystery Socrates in some sense reveals is the genuine mystery of nature. Its being secret does not depend on some convention that makes it unlawful to speak about. Instead, the genuine mystery of nature always withdraws from articulation, resists being put into words. *Nature loves to hide,* Heraclitus said. But the *Symposium* suggests that to a degree, or in a way, that mystery can be divined—but it suggests that in a way that is itself mysterious, true to the hidden ways of nature.

A third event in time complicates the chronology of the *Symposium*. In his speech at the party, Socrates takes his audience back to an earlier event in his life: he reports that he learned something of primary importance when he was younger, around 440 it seems, when he was about thirty years old.

Why is 440 significant?

What Socrates says about this event of learning shows that it must have occurred after 450, when Parmenides refuted Socrates' view of transcendent ideas. What Socrates here reports learning can be seen as a solution to the problem he was left with by Parmenides' refutation. Because the story that Socrates tells about the event of 440 comes after Parmenides' refutation of the ideas, it completes the three stages of Socrates' philosophic education.

That fact of completion in 440 tells us something else that is important: Socrates had already completed his philosophic education *before* the *Protagoras* in 434, in which Plato shows Socrates first mounting the public stage. Socrates' *philosophic* education came before his education in *political philosophy* that Plato set out in the three dialogues I discussed in the previous lecture, dialogues set in 434 and 429.

Back in 416 at the drinking party, Socrates says something very important for his coming speech after they have decided on the topic for their speeches: "I claim to have expert knowledge of nothing but erotics" (177d). *Erotics* are the things of eros, experienced first as a profound human passion of love or attraction that the Greeks elevated to a god. All the speeches of the *Symposium* are offered in praise of Eros, but Socrates' speech is the speech of a self-proclaimed knower, the speech of an already famous and celebrated philosopher who claims that this is the single thing of which he has expert knowledge. Socrates is famous for claiming ignorance, but in the *Symposium* he introduces himself as a knower with expert knowledge of what all the others are also going to make speeches about. Those others make up a very special group: they are among the most sophisticated knowers in highly sophisticated Athens, they are a special intellectual/spiritual few and each will speak as an expert. This is the most distinguished audience that Plato will ever show us for a speech by Socrates.

So the drinking party in 416 is a private gathering of special men, all in their way men of the Greek enlightenment. Instead of drinking they spend the party making speeches about the god Eros—and they dismiss the flute girls. It's just them, for private speeches among the enlightened few. In 416 Socrates is about fifty-three years old, fully mature. He speaks sixth or last, and only *after* that speech does Alcibiades *arrive*, late and drunk, and he makes a speech in praise of Socrates. Alcibiades is absent for the greatest of all speeches by Socrates.

Socrates starts his speech speaking as he usually does; he examines and refutes the view of Eros that Agathon, their host, just gave. Socrates brings Agathon to a point of perplexity, of admitting that he does not know what he thought he knew and had talked about so beautifully. That is, Socrates does young Agathon *the favor* of showing him his actual ignorance, his need for knowledge where he wrongly believed he already had it. Then he does Agathon another great favor: he says that he too was once put in that same state of neediness by a wise teacher who then led him, with the help of his own persistent questioning, to genuine knowledge of eros. Socrates' speech to everyone present is especially for one person, that brilliant young writer of tragedy who had just won the prize for tragedy. Socrates suggests to him that there's more than prize-winning; it's possible to grasp, on his own, the true understanding of eros that he wrongly thought he already had, but achieving that *more* depends on him, depends on him questioning as Socrates questioned.

Socrates tells Agathon that his teacher was a wise woman named Diotima and that when she led him to perplexity, he then questioned her and she taught him the essential lessons about Eros—and Socrates reports some of his conversations with Diotima.

What Socrates learned in 440

The first thing Diotima does with Socrates is refute his view, a view that was also Agathon's, that Eros is beautiful and good and wise. But Eros is not ugly or bad or ignorant. Instead, Diotima teaches Socrates that there is a *between* between the extremes of beautiful and ugly, and good and bad, and wisdom and ignorance. By beginning with what lies between wisdom and ignorance, Diotima begins her account of eros where the philosopher always begins. She first speaks of this between as "correct opinion"—that is the common way of occupying the *between* between wisdom and ignorance. Philosophy too occupies that between but occupies it differently. Neither wise nor ignorant, the philosopher experiences the passion for wisdom, he is *driven* to remedy his lack of wisdom: the philosopher occupies the between *erotically*, he is passionate to have what he knows he lacks.

Socrates' speech in the *Symposium* thus begins with *extremes* as he had begun in the *Parmenides*, where the extremes were the ideas and the particulars, or we could say, pure permanence and pure flow. The *Symposium* goes on to show how philosophy, driven erotically, can best think the reality that lies between those abstractions of permanence and flow, the reality that the philosopher in fact *is* as erotic, *is* as one particular in the totality of particulars. The philosopher can come to know by knowing himself.

Diotima then teaches Socrates that Eros is not a god but something between a god and a mortal. Taught to get over his shock at Eros not being a god, Socrates asks Diotima what such a between can *be* and what kind of *power* eros has. The power of *ferrying*, Diotima replies, the power of mediating or carrying things between the immortals and the mortal. This representation seems to imply that the power of eros is constantly generating mortal approximations of immortality. Diotima here seems to be in the realm of *the mythic*, in a kind of *theology* by means of which the fundamental condition or the fundamental human condition is represented by myths that account for that condition. Certainly what Socrates asks next leads Diotima to a most illuminating *mythic* picture of eros. Who is his father? And who is his mother? Socrates asks. That is, what are the origins of eros?

Diotima answers with a myth about the birth of Eros. A myth can only suggest or point to things to be thought about rationally. Myth must be followed by reasoning about what the myth suggests, and Diotima does go on to supply that reasoning. I will deal most extensively with the myth and then take up one feature only of her reasoning.

According to Diotima's myth, on the day Aphrodite, the goddess of sexual love, was born, the gods held a feast. Present at the feast was *Poros* or *Resource*, the son of Intelligence. And Penia, *Poverty*, came to the feast to beg. Resource got drunk and lay down in the Garden of Zeus. Poverty was plotting to have a child by Resource because she lacked resources, and she lay down beside him in the garden and conceived Eros. Strauss draws his main conclusion about the myth, or about the *Symposium* as a whole, from Poverty's *plotting*, her planning, her calculating. Plotting Poverty shows that she cannot be simply ignorant: she knew what she lacked and she wanted to have it and she acted to get it. Poverty, we see, is *resourceful*; she does not lack intelligence. Strauss says: "Eros, I conclude, resembles only his mother"—because eros too is resourceful poverty. Eros and his mother have the same essential quality of resourceful poverty. The myth suggests that the parent of *eros* is eros. As Francis Bacon concluded on this very point, *Eros has no parents*—and that is the greatest thing, Bacon says. And Plato too seems to be saying that: it is the greatest thing that eros has no parents and that we can know that eros has no parents. Eros springs from eros and eros results in eros.

George Dunn has a nice word for that: he says that eros is *auto-poietic*, self-making in Greek, self-generating—eros as self-generating never simply *is* but is always coming into being as a result of its own activity and always slipping out of being as a result of its self-expenditure, its dying away in its expressing itself.

Seth Benardete makes the same point about eros, and he adds a helpful generalization about Platonic myth: myth splits into *two* what is actually *one*, and that splitting displays the complex structure of the one so that we can, after learning from the splitting, go back to the one now knowing the internal structure of the one. Eros is one and has a complex structure. In Benardete's words, Eros is need and neediness (awareness of need); Eros is "self-aware desire." And Benardete emphasizes a second, indispensable matter: the deep structure of eros always disappears into the concrete experience that it enables: that always present disappearing is what makes eros essentially elusive; eros is in principle elusive because the deep structure of eros is always masked in the particular that it always disappears into.

So that's the primary conclusion about the always masked: Eros is desire or drive with an internal structure. The myth suggests that the structure of eros is to have a direction or impetus built into it as what it is: in being what it is, it is dynamic and directed out beyond itself toward that for which it is eros. The myth therefore suggests that the conclusion be expanded in a way that Benardete suggests: in its dynamic structure eros is always in a relation, always related to something outside it, as Penia desires to mate with Resource in order to produce offspring.

And the myth suggests yet another conclusion: its dynamic of always being in a relation gives it an always temporal aspect, it is always stretched out in time toward some future having. We can bundle all three aspects of this conclusion and say that the myth suggests that the internal structure of desire makes it always *dynamic*, *relational*, and *temporal*.

By splitting the mother of Eros from Eros and giving them the same quality, the myth suggests that the origin of desire is desire, and that the outcome of desire is desire. Backward toward its origins and forward toward its outcomes, eros is always desire directed by its very nature to fulfillment or satisfaction, and its fulfillment always drains away and revives seeking fulfillment.

I have to add a word about *fulfillment*. And that means reaching outside the myth to touch the main point of Diotima's reasoning after she tells the myth. The first stage of her argument considers eros as desire for the beautiful, but Socrates can't answer her question about what the fulfillment of that would mean. So she moves to consider eros as desire for the good, and the fulfillment of *that* Socrates can answer in a series of steps: ultimately, desire for the good is fulfilled in the happiness of the good's being one's own forever. But the difficulty of the *forever* leads Diotima to her final formulation of the fulfillment of eros: "begetting in the beautiful." Begetting in the beautiful is the *Symposium*'s ultimate definition of the fulfillment of eros. But Diotima makes it clear that this fulfillment always wanes or dies away, while eros always renews itself. With respect to the origins of eros I used George Dunn's word *auto-poietic* or self-generating. With the fulfillment of eros, its end or goal, I can use his word *auto-telic*, or having its goal, its *telos*, in itself as begetting or giving birth. So the myth suggests that the origin of eros is eros. And the reasoning suggests that the end or fulfillment of eros is eros.

Putting all this together, we can see that wise Diotima taught Socrates the ultimate philosophic lesson, a lesson that begins in a philosopher's self-knowledge as an erotic and extends out to the whole of what is as erotic. When Socrates says that he has "expert knowledge of nothing but erotics," he seems to make a modest or moderate knowledge claim; but in fact he makes a giant knowledge claim, the largest of all possible knowledge claims: he has expert knowledge of the character or way of all that is. Strauss states this comprehensive conclusion this way in his book *On Plato's Symposium*: "Eros, we can say, is the heart of coming into being and perishing. Eros, we can say, is the nature of nature."

What Diotima leads Socrates to is the intelligible character of the whole of what is. She leads Socrates to an *ontology*, a reasoned conclusion about beings as a whole: to be is to be eros and nothing else. The ontology Diotima suggests is therefore an ontology of "the sovereignty of becoming," to use Nietzsche's words, where becoming has the intelligible character of eros. It is a thing worthy of wonder and of gratitude that the totality has an intelligible structure that can be known by humans existing within it.

If we step back and interpret this lesson in the *Symposium* as one part of what Plato presents as Socrates becoming Socrates, we can see the coherence of the story Plato tells, or rather, intentionally *obscures* by scattering it across three dialogues. When the three stages are put together, the meaning of the *Symposium*'s final stage becomes clear as the completion of the first two stages. Plato put the first stage in the *Phaedo*, where he has Socrates on his last day tell the story of his beginnings in philosophy: he began where the Greek philosophers before him began, with the question of *cause* concerning generation and destruction as a whole. The *range* of Socrates' concern did not shrink to the human things alone when he struck out on his own with his turn to the speeches or accounts. Instead, that second sailing provided him with the route that took him first to transcendent ideas as the cause of all generation and decay. But Plato showed in the second stage, the *Parmenides* stage, that this first solution to the problem of cause by the nineteen-year-old Socrates fell victim early to Parmenides' proof of the rational impossibility of transcendent ideas. The third or *Symposium* stage of Socrates' philosophic education solves the problem of cause by resolving the problem set by Parmenides. What Socrates chose to present as what he learned from Diotima was the proper way to understand cause: what *is* lies in a *between* between pure flow and the pure fixity or permanence of the ideas; everything that *is* has the dynamic, relational, temporal character of *eros*. Socrates' expert knowledge of the erotic things is ultimately knowledge of the cause concerning generation and destruction as a whole. The *Symposium* completes Plato's story of Socrates' becoming Socrates because it shows his solution to the problem of cause with which he began. That solution answers philosophy's ultimate question, the question of the being of beings or the nature of nature.

The route to this knowledge passes through the self-knowledge of the philosopher, he lives erotically or passionately in the *between*, between wisdom and ignorance. That the erotic *between* of the philosopher can ultimately be seen as a guide to the erotic between-ness of all things helps us understand what Socrates said so often: *Know thyself.* That command, put up at Delphi as the god's command, has a special meaning for the philosopher. Through knowing himself as erotic he gets his clearest, nearest glimpse of what is true of all things: all beings exist in a way that is similar to the way that the highest, the most intellectual/spiritual being exists. Self-knowledge and then knowledge of the human as such is the route to the knowledge of the beings.

Now let's think again about the chronology that Plato built in to the *Symposium*. It begins in 399, just before Socrates' trial, and it takes us back to 416, when Socrates tells the tale of his ultimate learning, which occurred around 440. 416 is the time of the great Athenian crime of the profaning of the mysteries of Athenian religion. Could Plato be suggesting that Socrates committed the crime of *profaning* the genuine mysteries, the highest secrets of the philosophers and the secret of the being of beings? No, because Plato wrote the *Symposium*: if Socrates is a criminal for saying it, Plato is a worse criminal for writing it. No, Plato suggests something else by his complicated chronology of linking the time of discovering the truth of the ultimate mysteries, the time of the crime of profaning the religious mysteries, and the time of Socrates' trial. Plato suggests that Socrates, discoverer of the genuine mysteries, treated those mysteries, the mysteries hardest to know but knowable, in the way appropriate to them. And if *we* put Socrates on trial and test what he is saying, then we too can discover that Socrates—and Plato—treated the genuine mysteries in the proper way, a way that is itself hard to know but knowable. Unlike those criminals who profaned the religious mysteries, criminals that may include Alcibiades, Socrates treated the genuine mysteries appropriately: Socrates provided a way to be *initiated* into the mysteries, a way that initiates into the true secrets of nature those who pay him the closest attention. That initiation is suggested by what Socrates did first when it came time for him to speak: he refuted Agathon or led Agathon to perplexity; he gave Agathon the gift of knowing that if he was ever to know what eros is he had to begin again.

And the way for him to begin is the way Socrates began by asking Diotima. Can Agathon do that? Can he think through the stages that Diotima took the questioning Socrates through?—Socrates who seems to have been about Agathon's age when he began questioning Diotima. Only if he does that, only if Socrates becomes *his* Diotima, can he come to know what Socrates knows. And he will know *that* because he has in a way learned it on his own. In Plato's *Sym-*

posium Socrates does not betray the mysteries but prepares an initiation into them. And by writing the *Symposium* Plato makes Socrates, the instrument of Agathon's possible initiation, available for all future Agathons, for you and me. For our initiation.

There's one last thing that Diotima says in the *Symposium* that I want to be the last thing I say about Socrates becoming Socrates. Diotima has led Socrates to the ontological insight that is the final stage of philosophy: to be is to be eros. After leading Socrates to this insight, she makes a very long speech that is the last thing she says. Her long speech describes a ladder whose rungs or steps she climbs upward until she reaches the highest peak. She describes what happens at that peak as both *a seeing* and *a doing*. The one who has climbed to the peak *beholds* or *sees* perfect beauty, and that one *gives birth* or engages in a kind of *making* or *poetizing* in the presence of the beautiful. *Two* things happen at the peak, a beholding and an engendering or giving birth, a seeing and a making. And I end my lecture "Socrates Becomes Socrates" on *that* because in the last stage of Nietzsche's becoming Nietzsche something remarkably similar happens. He too will describe a beholding or seeing and he too will speak of an engendering or making that is its natural consequence. In both Plato and Nietzsche *philosophy*, seeing, leads to *philosophic poetry*, making.

And Strauss understood that; he says in his Nietzsche essay that Nietzsche's "fundamental proposition" is that "life is will to power or seen from within the world is will to power and nothing else," and he says next: "The will to power takes the place which the *eros* . . . occupies in Plato's thought." And Strauss shows how Nietzsche's philosophic insight into that fundamental or ontological matter led in

Nietzsche's religion chapter to an engendering, a making or a poetizing of the new highest ideal.

Plato and Nietzsche belong together: in becoming themselves philosophers become akin; they are of one kind; they see what is and what they see is of course similar or shared *because* it is a seeing of what is.

And each philosopher generates a teaching out of what he sees being to be. And the teaching each generates is *different* because a teaching must fit its times, must be ministerial in an effective way that depends on a true understanding of the times. Because times change, the teachings of the philosophers differ. The teachings of the philosophic kin Plato and Nietzsche differ radically, they stand in warring opposition to one another. That is as it must be: for the new to be established, all one hundred and eight suitors must die.

LECTURE 5

Nietzsche Becomes Nietzsche

Nietzsche is the subject of my last two lectures, and with Nietzsche I'm on home territory. It was from Nietzsche, not from Strauss, that I first learned what a philosopher is and what a philosopher can know. Those events of learning came with my study of *Thus Spoke Zarathustra*, particularly of "The Dance Song." There I first learned that Nietzsche laid claim to an ontology, an understanding of the being of beings, and that first learning was confirmed by my further study of Nietzsche's works, beginning with the chapter of *Zarathustra* called "On Self-Overcoming," in which Zarathustra reports his discovery in the Dance Song to one audience only, "you wisest." What I learned from Nietzsche was confirmed by my later study of Strauss, who also points to Nietzsche's ontology, and by my later study of Plato and of Bacon and Descartes. My Nietzsche lectures reflect my debt to Nietzsche and my alignment with Nietzsche, and the way that both Strauss and Plato further that alignment.

When the master author Plato constructs his dialogues in a way that allows you to discover that Socrates *becoming* Socrates is a theme that Plato himself wants his dedicated reader to pay attention to, *you pay attention*. My Plato lectures were meant to show that Plato structured his dialogues very artfully to allow you to discover the two basic aspects of Socrates' becoming: his becoming a *philosopher* and his becoming a *philosophic poet*.

My Nietzsche lectures are concerned with Nietzsche becoming Nietzsche. At an important point in his philosophic life, Nietzsche made his own becoming a theme for his reader. That is, he saw that he had to explain his becoming, he had to turn *autobiographical* and write about "Herr Nietzsche," "Mr. Nietzsche," even though, as a philosopher, he was naturally solitary, naturally a hermit whose private thinking was what mattered most. So in emphasizing Nietzsche's becoming, I'm following what Nietzsche himself encouraged his reader to do.

Nietzsche began to make his becoming public only at a certain point in his philosophic life. After finishing the two greatest books of his maturity, *Thus Spoke Zarathustra* and *Beyond Good and Evil*, he spent the second half of the year 1886 writing new *Forewords* to his previous books. He intended those Forewords to show how those books trace the progress of his thinking until he gained his mature thought in *The Gay Science*, his 1882 book, written just before *Zarathustra*. Then, two years after these autobiographical Forewords, late in 1888, as he was planning to publish his major new work, he published a whole book, *Ecce Homo—Behold the Man*—that was autobiographical. It was intended to show that he had won the right to publish the decisive, history-making book that would come next and that he never got to finish.

And there is another fact that points to the importance of Nietzsche's becoming: he thought of *Thus Spoke Zarathustra* as his most important published book, and that book was written to show Zarathustra's becoming, the stages of thought that he moved through to reach his mature position. And Zarathustra's becoming is a poetized version of Nietzsche's becoming: *Thus Spoke Zarathustra* is itself a version of Nietzsche's autobiography.

Before getting to Nietzsche's becoming, I want to say something about his relation to his philosophic predecessors, about whom he is *very critical*, singling out for special criticism, the ancient philosopher Plato and the modern philosopher Rousseau, the two philosophers he held most responsible for what Western philosophy and Western culture had become in his own time. At the very end of what he originally intended to be the second and final volume of *Human, All Too Human* he placed a very special section, number 408 of *Assorted Opinions and Maxims* (*Vermischte Meinungen und Sprüche*):

> I too have been to the underworld, like Odysseus, and will be there many times again. . . . There have been four pairs who do not refuse themselves to me . . . Epicurus and Montaigne, Goethe and Spinoza, Plato and Rousseau, Pascal and Schopenhauer. . . . Whatever I say, decide, think through for myself and others, upon these eight I fix my eyes and find theirs fixed on me.

In this amazing reflection, Nietzsche shows that *this* is who he is, *this* is where he belongs, among the thinkers of the highest rank. He visits these eight thinkers in the underworld; they are all dead but live on, alive in their works. What Nietzsche pictures himself doing is what Homer's Odysseus did, descend to the underworld, where the first figure he met was the wise man *Teiresias*—and Odysseus learned from Teiresias his own task as a wise ruler. In the underworld of the wise to which Nietzsche descends, his special eight are his Teiresiases. And they include Plato and Rousseau, the two philosophers he most criticizes. What he says about his eight is that whatever he *says, decides, thinks through for himself and others*, "upon these eight I fix my eyes and find theirs fixed on me." Nietzsche put this statement at the very end of *Human, All Too Human*, the book that began his attempt to win complete freedom for his mind. And those three verbs, *saying*, *deciding*, and *thinking through for himself and others*, do not say that he takes his *thinking* from them. His thinking is different from his *thinking through for myself and others* (in German, his *denken* is different from his *andenken für mich und andere*). Nietzsche's *thinking* is wholly his own. Working to become *wholly free in his thinking*, he takes his *standard of action* from the history of great thinkers and actors who have determined the spiritual and intellectual course of the West.

Nietzsche lives and acts in the presence of the greatest thinkers. They are the standard by which he determines his own doings and he knows that their doings determined the history of the West. Nietzsche lives and acts as the latest one of those and measures himself by them and sees them measuring him.

Nietzsche thought very highly of himself. And he had every right to do so. He knew himself.

I want to make a second general point about Nietzsche and his books: In his autobiography, *Ecce Homo*, he called all his books from *Beyond Good and Evil* on, "*fishhooks*." He explained his use of *fishhook* in letters: his books were intended to *catch* those readers he really wants, the few "who are related" to him. They would be drawn to him for further instruction in a philosophical school that would be like the ancient Greek schools of philosophy. He imagined establishing such a school while he was writing *Human, All Too Human* in 1876–8. His reason was that not everything can be said in books; and training in philosophy could be conducted best in a small school of the like-minded. Nietzsche never got to establish such a school, so the books have to stand by themselves. Still, even as fishhooks Nietzsche wrote his books to be a schooling, to teach his reader how to read and how to think.

That Nietzsche thought of his books as fishhooks already indicates the presence of the *exoteric/esoteric distinction* in his work. Nietzsche spoke of that distinction most explicitly in *Beyond Good and Evil.* It comes early in the second chapter, "The Free Mind," just after he has said that there are *exceptions* to the rule that everyone is satisfied with the "simplifications and falsifications" with which almost all people live. There are exceptions to that rule who want to know the truth. But not only that, there are *exceptions among the exceptions* who want to know exactly how they differ from everyone else in their thinking: they "go down" to examine others and they "go inside" to know themselves. They do what Socrates did. To readers prepared in this way by the first sections of The Free Mind, he then speaks of the exoteric and the esoteric in *Beyond Good and Evil* #30:

> Our highest insights must—and should!—sound like follies, possibly like crimes, when they come without permission to the ears of those who are not the kind for them, not predestined for them.

Our highest insights, that is, the insights of the exception among the exceptions, the philosopher, whose drive it is to know and to know himself. Non-philosophers will judge the philosopher to be a madman or a criminal if *his* insights come to *their* ears, the ears of those who are not the kind for them—Socrates had said the exact same thing in Plato's *Republic.* Nietzsche then says that this is an old and well-known view:

> The difference between the exoteric and the esoteric as one formerly among philosophers distinguished them among the Indians as among the Greeks, Persians, and Muslims. . . .

Nietzsche's good friend, the scholar of Sanskrit philosophy, Paul Deussen, introduced Eastern philosophy to Germany. He answered Nietzsche's questions about Indian philosophy, and may have later informed him about *Chinese philosophy,* but Nietzsche knew very little about it.

Nietzsche's sentence on exotericism goes on to say what the distinction between exoteric and esoteric does *not* mean: It is not a distinction between the outside and inside, as if you could pass from outside to inside just by being told something or whispered something. Instead, he says,

> the much more essential is that [the exoteric approach] views things from below and the esoteric down from above.

The exception among exceptions looks down from a very high height—from a perspective that you have to *work* to achieve. The exception among exceptions has won a privileged viewpoint that you cannot share unless you climb to that height yourself. Still, Nietzsche can *report* what he sees from there:

> There are heights of the soul where, to look out from which, tragedy itself ceases to have a tragic effect, and taking all the woe of the world together, who may dare to decide whether its sight *necessarily* seduces and compels precisely to pity and thus to doubling the woe?

Nietzsche's report from above simply *says* that the exception among exceptions, the philosopher, looking down from above on tragedy, does not feel the standard effects of tragedy, which are pity and fear. Tragedy remains tragedy; life is not transformed in the view from above. The *effect* of tragedy is different.

The second part of what I just read expands tragedy to *the whole of human suffering* and asks: who may dare to decide that the view from above necessarily leads to *pity* for the human, that is, to the great modern virtue, pity? *Who* may dare? The answer must be the exception among the exceptions, the philosopher. He *now* dares that. Because he has the privileged viewpoint, down from above, Nietzsche faces the profound question of whether to take pity on suffering humanity, to view humanity's tragic fate, and consequently—although Nietzsche does not say this here—feel the responsibility to offer humanity some *deliverance*, some *redemption* or other. That is what the fact of the exoteric/esoteric distinction results in for Nietzsche—will the philosopher *today* generate a teaching that will cover over the tragedy, the totality of suffering, and make it seem bearable because there is some deliverance, as philosophers in the Platonic tradition have taught till now? Or does the philosopher now judge that the time has come for a new response to the view from above, down on human suffering? Is it time for a new teaching that does not lie about suffering by inventing or endorsing some comedy of a purpose to existence that gives suffering meaning? Nietzsche's answer is that, yes, the time has come for such a new teaching. A notebook entry from 1888, two years later, puts one aspect of that conclusion in a way that condemns all of the platonic teachers:

> We're proud not to have to be liars any more, or slanderers, or discreditors of life.

The philosophic tradition of exoteric noble lying comes to a self-conscious end with Nietzsche. He's proud not to have to be a liar. It's easy for me to imagine that right here Nietzsche felt the eyes of his underworld judges on him for not continuing what Plato called the "noble" lie. And Nietzsche knows how extremely dangerous that is, because it opens up exposure to fundamental truths that he himself called "true but deadly" (the sovereignty of becoming, the fluidity of all concepts, types, and kinds, the lack of any cardinal difference between man and the animals). (It is worthwhile to note again that the "deadly" truths are not deadly to Nietzsche; he judges them deadly to society based on a belief in a purpose of existence for human beings.)

As I will emphasize, the Nietzsche who is proud not to have to be a liar any more *does* have an exoteric teaching. The exoteric/esoteric distinction still means for Nietzsche what it meant for Plato in this sense: in Nietzsche, too, genuine philosophy generates philosophic poetry; in Nietzsche's language, philosophy generates *art*. And the poetry or art that philosophy generates in Nietzsche can be given a label that derives from Leo Strauss: the ultimate art in Nietzsche is a theological-political teaching—philosophic poetry.

So those are the themes of the rest of my Nietzsche lectures: Nietzsche is a genuine philosopher who lives on in the underworld with the other great philosophers; and Nietzsche, the philosopher, continues the exoteric/esoteric tradition of philosophy but in a new way.

I'm now writing a new book on Nietzsche, on how Nietzsche *became* Nietzsche. The topic of Nietzsche's becoming has not been adequately treated in Nietzsche studies partly because Strauss's recovery of the exoteric/esoteric distinction has not been applied to Nietzsche. My new book does apply that distinction and aims to set out Nietzsche's genuine becoming. For the rest of this lecture I will give an outline of Nietzsche's becoming and then a more detailed outline of what he actually became.

Nietzsche's 1876 turn

In his first five books (1872–1876) Nietzsche put himself in the service of others, of Schopenhauer and Wagner; those books are *pre-Nietzschean* books, although they contain a great deal that is important for really knowing Nietzsche. Then, in the summer of 1876, Nietzsche made a decisive *turn*; he turned away from the perspective of his first five books to take his own path in philosophy, the path to achieve a free mind, as he called it. Freeing the mind has one aim above all others, to discover the truth; the way to the truth passes through an understanding of the ways in which the mind is unfree or "prejudiced." In the very first book of what became a series of books on freeing the mind, Nietzsche quoted Descartes "In Place of a Foreword," and what he quoted was Descartes's own statement on his turn to the philosophic life. Nietzsche's 1876 turn can be regarded as his *turn to the philosophic life.*

Freeing the mind meant for Nietzsche studying the *human soul* with knowledge of his own soul, *self-knowledge*, as a crucial component: how do the drives and passions of the soul influence or prejudice human understanding? It also meant studying *human culture* in its history from human beginnings through the high culture of the Greeks in which he had his professional training: how did culture build bias and prejudice into human understanding? It also meant studying the *history of philosophy*, studying his great predecessors to see how their teachings influenced the particular perspectives or prejudices of western culture; in particular, it meant studying Kant and his followers in order to understand how the faculties of perception and cognition place essential limits on the capacity of the human mind to know the world.

And crucially for him in the second half of the nineteenth century in Europe, it meant using all the resources of *modern science,* which had been advancing knowledge and publicizing it since the beginnings of the Enlightenment almost three centuries earlier, and which had made solid progress with strict methods of gaining and communicating knowledge: modern science with its dependable findings was a now indispensable part of freeing the mind. Nietzsche strongly criticized the education he had gotten because it had not given him a grounding in the sciences of physics and chemistry and anthropology. (After completing *Thus Spoke Zarathustra* Nietzsche planned to go to a University to study *physics* for five years.)

So there was a lot for Nietzsche to do after his decisive turn in 1876 to *gain* a free mind and at the same time to *teach the ideal* of the free mind—to win other talented minds for this project of understanding.

Nietzsche continued to publish books while following his path to a free mind. The first of those books, *Human, All Too Human* in 1878, he subtitled *A Book for Free Minds*. Then he published a separate book with the same title but as an *Appendix* or *Addition* in 1879; and in 1880 he published *The Wanderer and His Shadow*, a book with the same aim. Then his project of freeing the mind took the focus that he would maintain to the end, the focus first gained in the book *Daybreak* in 1881. He viewed that book as a new beginning for him, what he called his "campaign against morality." Having come to understand the power of morality and its dangerous and negative effects, his study of morality extended to a war against it.

After he finished *Daybreak*, he started again as he always did, with a *new notebook* in which he wrote entries intended for his next book. He thought that the entries would prepare a second book called *Daybreak*, chapters 6 through 10. But when he finally published that new book it had only four chapters and had the title, *The Gay Science*. In the fourth chapter of that book he reported his decisive breakthrough that he had first written out in his notebook. I take this breakthrough on the path of freeing his mind to be Nietzsche's decisive step into his maturity. With book 4 of *The Gay Science*, Nietzsche became Nietzsche.

The 1881 turn

Nietzsche gave a sign of his breakthrough in a Notice that he put on the back cover of the first edition of *The Gay Science* when it appeared in the summer of 1882. That notice reads:

> With this book a series of writings by Friedrich Nietzsche comes to its end, the writings whose common goal it is to erect a new image and ideal of the free mind.

And then he listed the books in this series from *Human, All Too Human* to *The Gay Science*. So the great project of Nietzsche's 1876 turn, to erect a new image and ideal of the free mind, is *over* in 1882; he *completed it* successfully. Nietzsche's free mind had reached the goal that the whole free mind project existed to reach: the truth, fundamental truth that freeing his mind had aimed at from the start. So erecting the ideal of the free mind could no longer be his highest ideal any more. Now his books could have a different aim: *showing what the free mind can come to know*, showing the truth that the freed mind can rightly *tie* itself to, rightly *bind* itself to—*because* it's the truth. And that's what Nietzsche's next books do: *Thus Spoke Zarathustra* and *Beyond Good and Evil* lead the reader into the truth Nietzsche discovered.

So this turn, the 1881 turn that Nietzsche first made public in book 4 of *The Gay Science* is the decisive turn in his life. What had Nietzsche discovered, what truths had he gained, that made this turn possible? That's what both my Nietzsche lectures are about: what Nietzsche's free mind discovered and what his books from then on were written to introduce.

The notebook with the new discoveries

To show what Nietzsche discovered it seems best to me to go back to the writing in which Nietzsche first wrote out those discoveries. That writing is the new notebook he began in March, 1881, just after completing *Daybreak*; he filled that notebook with entries from the spring of 1881, through the summer and into the fall. Then he composed much of *The Gay Science* from entries in that notebook. *The Gay Science* contains the new discoveries *in the form* Nietzsche wanted them to have in their first public presentation. He never intended that anyone ever read the notebook in which he first wrote them out; that was private, for him alone. Luckily for us, however, Nietzsche's sister Elisabeth preserved that notebook and every other scrap of writing by her brother, and she established the Nietzsche Archive to make them permanently available to scholars. And she began the project of publishing those private notes.

Before looking into that 1881 notebook, I want to say something about Nietzsche's notebooks generally. They are like the notebooks of no one else for this reason: Nietzsche suffered from very bad eyesight from birth that included extreme near-sightedness. While he was composing *Human,*

All Too Human in 1876 and 1877, one aspect of his bad eyesight got much worse: his eyes became even more sensitive to light, with the result that he could read or write for only about one and a half hours each day before it caused extreme headaches. That is a disaster for a thinker whose thinking life is furthered by reading and writing. In order to save the one thing he lived for, Nietzsche devised a practice that he followed for the rest of his writing life. He described it in a letter to his best friend. For six to eight hours every day he would take long walks. On those walks he composed his thoughts, and his arguments, and his images, composed them into sentences and paragraphs while he was walking. After his six to eight hours of walking, he returned to his room, usually a single room he rented in some rooming house. There he wrote out his already composed paragraphs in the large notebook that he kept in his room. Except for the ones from near the end of his writing life, these notebooks are very orderly, written in steady handwriting on almost every line of the lined pages. The entries are not random; they are not scattered thoughts hurriedly written down; they are already polished paragraphs, long and short, that he had composed while walking. Then, in the later stages of composing a book from his notebook entries, Nietzsche would organize and assemble these already coherent paragraphs into ordered themes and chapters, editing and rewriting the entries, adding and subtracting, until he had arranged the entries into whole chapters. Especially in the later books, each chapter is a disciplined sequence with a beginning, middle, and end.

The 1881 notebook that he began just after *Daybreak* and filled with material for *The Gay Science* seems to me the most important of all the notebooks. Its entries show Nietzsche in the process of discovering the two most important insights of his mature philosophy. And that's what the rest of my

Nietzsche lectures will be about: the two discoveries that made it possible to end the free mind series of books and begin the books of his maturity.

The 1881 notebook and *ontology*, an account of the being of beings

The 1881 notebook shows Nietzsche's thought advancing beyond his close focus on *morality*, with its popular division of human actions into *egoistic* and *altruistic*. Egoistic actions serve the self or the "I," altruistic actions serve the other or others. The prevailing morality judged egoistic actions mostly bad and altruistic actions mostly good. Already in *Daybreak*, Nietzsche judged that *all* human actions, including moral actions, are based on drives or passions that are in principle egoistic or self-serving. Every seemingly altruistic action actually fulfilled a veiled or hidden egoistic drive.

Nietzsche's investigation of the drives behind human actions belongs to *psychology* or the study of the human soul. It is a study of the actions of others but it is also, as philosophers at least since Socrates emphasized, the study of one's own soul, *self*-study, leading to self-knowledge. Nietzsche's growing investigation of the human, self-knowledge and knowledge of others, led him to the conclusion that the drives are not only egoistic, but that they all share a fundamental characteristic, they are all similar in one way and Nietzsche gave that way different names in the notebook. Listen to some of the words he used to describe this shared quality. My words are English translations of Nietzsche's German words; each is a compound word that the German language can build so easily into long single words:

Addiction to having. Wanting to have. Wanting to hold on to. Urge for property or ownership. Wanting to own. Drive for ownership. The passion to appropriate. The passion for power.

These compound words try to name *the drive itself*: addiction, urge, wanting, passion. And they try to name *the object* of the drive: having, holding on to, owning, appropriating, making into my property. Nietzsche used these compound words *first* to describe human actions, to try to give the right name to the feature he found present in all human actions, even if those actions don't seem to be what is named. Another aspect of that common drive comes up often in Nietzsche's notes: *love*. Love is a passion to possess and to possess all of the desired object.

Another main feature in Nietzsche's entries in the notebook puts the drives into an *order of rank* from lowest and most common to highest and rarest. His usual phrase for the highest of the drives is *the passion for knowledge*, what he recognized as his own most powerful passion, a passion not categorically different from the other passions but the peak of the passions, the *geistigste*, the most intellectual/spiritual, the top of the rank order of the passions.

Another main feature of these entries is that within the individual soul the drives exist in a constant war with one another for *supremacy*, or for *rule*.

The most important development in this notebook shows Nietzsche's thinking about morality and the drives basic to it moving in the direction in which philosophy always moves: from an understanding of the particular toward the more comprehensive. And this notebook shows Nietzsche arriving at the most comprehensive possible application of these words for the common feature of the drives of the human soul: the words describe what is true of all human actions; but more than that, they are true of all actions of all living things; and then comes the most comprehensive judgment: they are true of all actions of all things.

So *psychology*, knowledge of the human soul, including self-knowledge, expands to *biology*, knowledge of the organic, of all aliveness, and that expands to *physics*, knowledge of all beings and all actions: and in each of these fields, the same common property is the ultimate explanation of what is at work there. It is in this notebook that Nietzsche arrived at that ultimate expansion. He did not use philosophy's word for this, *ontology*, a word he avoided because of his suspicions about what he called "university philosophy." But we can use it as philosophy's word for the most comprehensive study, the study of *being* or of *the being of beings*, which is what the Greek word *ontology* literally means. Nietzsche arrived at his ontological conclusion in the 1881 notebook and named the drive present in all things the "addiction to have," *Habsucht* in German, the most common word Nietzsche used for it in the notebook.

It is important to say that within a year Nietzsche gave a different name to the fundamental phenomenon, because he had come to understand it better, differently and far more subtly. So he replaced the term *Habsucht* with the new comprehensive term, *Wille zur Macht*. The "addiction to have" he replaced with "will to power." The reason for the change was Nietzsche's continued push to understand the fundamental force ever more adequately. It was *not* basically a desire to have, as if possession of what was out there was what drove it. Instead, Nietzsche saw that what was basic was a desire to overcome; it was a force that reaches beyond itself and encounters the other in the form of *resistance*, and drives to overcome that resistance. And that other is not other in its essence; it too is a desire to overcome. So what is ultimately at work in all things is *force* that always exists within a *field* of forces. And Nietzsche decided that it was best named *will to power* because what it is is its need to discharge its excess of force against resistance which is itself force. And that was the name Nietzsche then used in *Thus Spoke Zarathustra* and all of his books after that. But Nietzsche clearly recognized the inadequacy of even that label, *will to power*. He called it a "weakening and limiting metaphor" (BGE 22), but no other term seemed to him to come as close to naming the fundamental phenomenon.

I want to be clear because I'm talking about *Nietzsche becoming Nietzsche*: I jumped from the ontology expressed in the 1881 notebook to the more adequate ontological insight and terminology that he first attained a year or so later. I did that to make clear from the start that he refined and improved the ontological insight of the 1881 notebook. But with that brief look at Nietzsche's ultimate ontological insight, I want to jump back to the 1881 notebook, because it is there that he first made the ontological step into an understanding of being as such.

So the 1881 notebook shows Nietzsche arriving at his comprehensive application of his explanatory principle of the human drives. And this 1881 notebook also shows Nietzsche arriving at his second crucial discovery, the one for which the notebook is well known among Nietzsche scholars: it records Nietzsche's discovery of *eternal return*, the teaching for which Nietzsche wanted to be known. That's what makes this 1881 notebook, after *Daybreak*, before *The Gay Science*, the most important of them all: it contains both of Nietzsche's most crucial thoughts, the thoughts through which Nietzsche entered his maturity as a philosopher. Gaining these two thoughts, Nietzsche became Nietzsche, became who he was.

Now I want to look at what Nietzsche, the writer of books, *did* with his achievement of an ontology in his 1881 notebook. He reported it first in *The Gay Science*, the book that made public all his main insights from the notebook. The structure of *The Gay Science* is important. Its first three chapters are very much like *Daybreak* in their investigations of morality and art and science. Nietzsche seems to have composed those chapters in January, 1882. But then he wrote a very different fourth chapter that he decided would be the last chapter. It was different from the first three for one reason only: he wrote that last chapter *after* he had decided in that January of 1882 that he would write a book called *Thus Spoke Zarathustra*, and *that book* would be a more complete report on the discoveries in his 1881 notebook. So before writing that most important book he would ever write, he finished *The Gay Science* by adding a last chapter very different from its first three. It is the only chapter with a title: *Sanctus Januarius* in Latin, "*Saint January*" in English.

January is the first month of the new year; it is a time for looking back over the old year and forward to the new year; and it is a time for judging your life and making resolutions for a better life. *Saint January* opens a new year in Nietzsche's thought; he titled its first section "*To the new year*" and made it his new year's resolution. Then he structured his chapter around his two new thoughts. The single most important thought, *the drive to possess*, he placed carefully just after the center, well prepared by the actual center. The second most important thought, *eternal return*, he placed very carefully at the end.

How *Saint January* introduced Nietzsche's ontology

Nietzsche prepared his most important section beautifully with the two sections that precede it. Just before the center is a section titled "*The history of every day*" and it asks *you*, in the singular familiar, how you spend your every day—Like everyone else? With their every day concerns of praise or blame or respectability? Or are you of a different sort, driven to examine the inside of things and of yourself? With this *you* Nietzsche singles out his genuine reader, the only reader he really wants. Here, for you, he baits his fishhook for the ones related to him.

Next comes his central section, called "*Out of the seventh solitude.*" Here, the "wanderer" who has overcome every obstacle faces an unexpected, final crisis—he stands in a garden, but it is a garden with a temptation: in this garden the wanderer can finally rest and believe he has attained his goal. But Nietzsche calls it "*Armida's garden,*" a literary reference that only a few will understand: *Armida's garden* is a temptation to *a man with a mission*, the great *Rinaldo* in the story; Rinaldo is tempted to stop just short of his ultimate achievement, conquest or capture of the Holy City. To achieve that most difficult final conquest *you* must tear yourself away from Armida's garden and strive for the truly ultimate gain. And when you see *that*, when you see what these two sections at the center do in singling *you* out and warning you of a last temptation, you know you're not making it up, you're finding what Nietzsche put there for you; you're not inventing some theory but are actually on your way to discovering the central matter.

After this careful preparation, Nietzsche placed the section he called, "*Will and wave.*" It begins with a poetic description of a wave, waves of the sort he often watched that winter of 1881–82, the waves of the Mediterranean Sea near the Italian city of Genoa where he wrote *Saint January*:

> How greedily this wave comes in, as if it had to reach something! How it creeps with terrifying haste on

> into the inmost crevices of the rocky cliff! It seems that it wants to beat someone to it, that there is something hidden that has value, high value. —And now it comes back, somewhat slower, still completely white from excitement,—is it disappointed? Did it find what it sought? Is it feigning disappointment? —But already another wave nears, greedier and wilder still than the first, and its soul too appears to be full of secrets and of the passions of treasure-hunting.

So there is the whole activity, the passionate drive forcing itself into the most hidden. And it falls back white with excitement. In *disappointment*? Or could it be *faking* disappointment? If it is faking disappointment, it *found what it sought*, it achieved its goal. Its achievement occurs in a *contest* of strivings for the hidden, because the next wave is already coming.

And Nietzsche then wrote,

> . . . That is how the waves live—that is how we live, we who will!—

"*Will and wave*" is the title; we the willful wanderers are like the waves, the waves are an image for what we are. Then Nietzsche added a resolution or vow, followed by a speech addressed to the waves themselves in the plural familiar:

> —more I won't say. —So, you distrust me? You are angry with me, you beautiful monsters? Are you afraid I will divulge your entire secret? . . . For—hear this well!—I know you and your secret; I know your kind!—You and I, we have indeed One secret!

This is Nietzsche's report for *you*, that singular reader whose every day is like his. You might be able to gain the secret that the willful share with the waves, but only if you too are a wanderer like him who can push on beyond Armida's garden to the ultimate gain.

What is that secret? *Will and wave* does not say: the last words I read are the last words of the section. Nietzsche does not tell the secret he shares with the waves; he does not betray, does not profane, his secret and the secret of the waves. He leaves it to be wondered about and figured out by you.

"More I won't say," Nietzsche said. But in the draft he wrote of "*Will and wave*" he wrote words that he decided not to publish, words he struck out. And those words go a long way in betraying the secret of what he shares with the waves. It's cheating to look at them, but here they are. After describing the *greediness* of the waves crashing into the rocky cliff and penetrating to the hidden, and then another wave coming, "greedier than the first and it too seems to be full of secrets and of the passions of treasure-hunting"—right after that Nietzsche spoke directly to the waves using two German words that I want to repeat in German:

> *Oh ihr Habsüchtigen, ihr Wissensgierigen.*

Those German words, *Habsüchtigen* and *Wissensgierigen*, *name* the secret of the waves, the secret that is also *his* secret. The first word, *Habsüchtigen*, is the German word for *possession addicts*, you who are *driven to possess, driven to have*. The second word, *Wissensgierigen*, means you who are *greedy to know*. So Nietzsche says to the waves, "Oh you *possession-addicts*, *you knowledge-greedy*." And he says *that* to the waves of the sea.

In the 1881 notebook, *possession-addiction* is Nietzsche's word for the quality or property that is present in all things or events—the word for the comprehensive or universal ontological drive. And *the greed to know* is a word for the passion for knowledge, the highest or supreme drive of the human way of being. So the two words name the drive of *all beings* and the drive of the *highest being*. In the published version of *Will and wave*, instead of saying to the waves, *Oh you possession-addicts, you knowledge-greedy*, Nietzsche says what I read, "So you mistrust me? . . . Are you afraid I will divulge your entire secret?" The published version keeps the secret as the draft version did not. The published version leaves it to *you* to figure out the secret of what you in your knowledge-seeking share with the waves crashing into the cliff and trying to force their way into every crack and corner of the cliff. The published version keeps the secret by putting it only in the poetry of the likeness of waves and the knowledge-seeker.

We are considering *Nietzsche becoming Nietzsche*, and this is the essential step in his becoming himself, his ontological insight. And *this* is how Nietzsche chose to make his first ever public indication that he had arrived at a conclusion about a comprehensive ontology, the hidden quality shared by all things from the waves of the sea to the driven inquirer. That is the beautiful form that Nietzsche chose for his first indication that he had arrived at the deepest insight a freed mind can gain. In publishing it this way Nietzsche took care to place it at the center of "*Saint January*"—the center contains the central matter and the central matter, the *ontology*, deserves to be treated in this indirect, secretive way. And remember, before Leo Strauss called everyone's attention to the center by insisting that that's where good writers hid their most important points, before Strauss made the center prominent, the center was the least prominent place in a writing, the place where one is most likely to have lost his focus in comparison with the attention he paid at the beginning and at the end. But *you*, the *you* Nietzsche actually spoke to in asking, How do *you* spend your every day?, *you* paid attention at the center because Nietzsche spoke it to you.

The 1881 notebook and *eternal return*

Now I want to consider the second of Nietzsche's two most basic discoveries, eternal return, and the way he chose to first make *that* public. If you continue to read the entries in the 1881 notebook after the ones that first state the ontological conclusion about addiction to possession and the similar ontological terms, you come almost immediately to the famous entry that is Nietzsche's first ever account of eternal return. Nietzsche himself made that entry famous by referring to it in his autobiography seven years later and making that notebook entry the first thing he said about *Thus Spoke Zarathustra* and even mentioning that he wrote it in his notebook. In the notebook it is the first *dated* entry, "the beginning of August, 1881." By dating it Nietzsche indicated its importance to him.

After that first ever entry on eternal return every entry for many pages concerns the new thought, and all of those, including the first, have one primary concern: *how to introduce* that thought. So it seems that Nietzsche first had the thought of eternal return on his walk and that it came as the overwhelming thought he reports it to be. But he didn't write down that experience itself in his notebook: the first entry is not about the overwhelming thought itself. Instead, it is a detailed, well-structured *book plan* that deals with the problem of how to introduce this thought to others.

The problem is this: eternal return appeared to Nietzsche as the new ideal, the opposite ideal to the one that shaped

Western culture and all other cultures since the beginning of what he called the moral period. How can a new ideal be introduced? How can an ideal opposite to the prevailing ideal be introduced? Who would ever believe it or value it or even take it seriously when it is so contrary to what we already believe?

The book plan in the notebook with Nietzsche's first ever mention of eternal return proposes five chapters, with eternal return appearing only in the last chapter. The book plan is orderly and rich and sets out conclusions that Nietzsche had been working toward for years. We don't have time to look at the whole plan, so I'll compress it all into the *one word* that is most important and that Nietzsche used constantly in connection with eternal return in the notebook. That word in English is *incorporation*, and the German word, *Einverleibung*, is identical in its structure. The first part, the *in* of *in*corporation, stands for *taking in*, a taking in to the *corpus* or the *body*. To *incorporate* is to take into your body—like taking in food which becomes a part of the body, bone, flesh, blood. The body is *formed* and *sustained* by what it takes in: the body is a product of *incorporation*.

Nietzsche was interested in the *physiological* or bodily aspects of incorporation and he took them to be basic. But he was more interested in the *spiritual* aspects of incorporation where the same kind of operation is at work. Nietzsche's German word is better than *spiritual* because that word, *geistig*, includes spiritual and *intellectual*, and with Nietzsche, of course, the intellectual is what counts most. So Nietzsche's first four chapters set out his view that to be a mature human being is *always already to be formed or stamped* by the inescapable processes of incorporation that have made us. A philosopher, that is, a thinker who has worked to free his mind, frees his mind of incorporated views as far as that is possible: among other things, his freed mind sees the necessary errors of *cultural* incorporation, of all the *ideals* and *values* we have taken in and made our own in our education and training: those ideals and values have *made* us what we are. But the freed mind of the philosopher also sees that the errors of cultural incorporation are subject to alteration; they can be changed because they have all been taught, and it is possible to teach different ideals and values, different from those already incorporated.

That's a summary of four/fifths of the book Nietzsche planned to write. My summary is meant to show the problem Nietzsche consciously faced in introducing his new ideal, his new highest value, as Strauss calls it. Because it's new it will necessarily sound strange and foreign and false to those who have already incorporated a different highest value; it will be unwelcome because it opposes what is already deeply incorporated as a way of thinking and believing. To be effective, a new ideal must *already* be incorporated, must be a part of what everyone *already* knows, what one has begun to know from the very beginning of one's conscious life. When the thought of eternal return first came to Nietzsche, he knew he faced the founder's abstract problem of introducing novelty into a culture that had already incorporated a different view.

Now, staying with the notebook, I move from the problem of incorporation to another important issue about eternal return. The first ever entry on eternal return *comes after* Nietzsche's comprehensive ontological conclusion. The chronological sequence in which Nietzsche wrote out the thoughts he arrived at on his walks shows that he *first* drew his ontological conclusion and *only then* did the ideal of eternal return come to him. And when you think about it, that is the only possible *rational sequence* for these two thoughts: *first* comes the comprehensive understanding of the way the world is, the way all beings are. *Only then* can the thought of eternal return arrive, because that thought says to the world now known: *that's what I want,* I want *that world,* the world *as it is,* and I want it *again,* and I want it all *an infinite number of times* again exactly as it is—because I want my life just as it is again.

Strauss recognized this connection between Nietzsche's two main thoughts: he called will to power "*the fundamental fact,*" and he called eternal return "*the highest value.*" The relationship between the two is the relationship between *fact and value.* So of course, *first* comes the fact, *then* comes the affirmation of the fact, the *yes* to that fact. The connection between fact and value is the connection between *understanding* the world and *loving* the world understood. And Strauss gave that connection its proper name: he called it Nietzsche's "*relapse into Platonism,*" a relapse that cannot be altogether avoided by the philosopher.

So that's what Nietzsche's 1881 notebook shows by the simple chronological sequence of its entries. It shows the philosopher Nietzsche coming to understand that to be is to be will to power and nothing else, and then, only then, glimpsing the new ideal of wanting that world, the world understood, to be an infinite number of times.

How *Saint January* introduced eternal return

Now I want to look again at *Saint January,* the final chapter of *The Gay Science,* in order to see how Nietzsche chose to present his eternal return discovery publicly for the first time. His chosen way of publicizing *that* is just as illuminating as his chosen way of publicizing his ontological discovery: *that* discovery he placed at the center of the chapter as a secret, challenging *you* to discover what you share with the waves. Nietzsche hid his ontological discovery at the center of his chapter. But he put his second discovery, his discovery of eternal return, at the end of the chapter, and he made it highly prominent, noticeable even by someone who leafed quickly to the end to see how this book would end.

At the end of *Saint January*, the end of *The Gay Science*, Nietzsche arranged a series of important sections; he ended in a *January* way, a way that fits a new year. First, he builds toward the end with a series of important sections that summarize his chief themes of morality, and then, in the third section from the end, he speaks of what is ending, the core teaching of the old year. In a section called "*The dying Socrates*" he makes Socrates ultimately responsible for the teaching that came to dominate western civilization, the teaching that life can only be suffered and that humans need to be redeemed from a life of suffering by a healing god: Nietzsche interprets the last words of the dying Socrates—I owe a cock to Asclepius—as saying that for life to be over is a blessing. But now, as that old year passes, the dying Socrates is dying, his ideal, his anti-life teaching is dying.

The next section, second from the last, promises what the new year will bring, the new teaching to replace the teaching of the dying Socrates. Its title is "*The heaviest weight*," and it announces the new teaching that will give things weight again, make things important again. And this section makes Nietzsche's *first ever* public announcement of eternal return. This section, the second from the end of Nietzsche's book, first introduces Nietzsche's new teaching for the new "year." That section again speaks to *you*, and it makes you think of a demon whispering to you in your solitude, saying to you that you will experience your life exactly as it is again and again, with nothing changed, nothing different, nothing better. The whole question of the section is: what will your reaction be? Would you curse the demon for saying something horrifying? Or would you say to him, "You are a god and never have I heard anything so divine"?

Then the scene changes, the demon is gone, and "this thought has gained power over you." In his first public announcement of his thought, Nietzsche here shifts to what concerned him in his notebook. The sudden announcement by the demon is replaced by what would happen to you if you had had the thought of eternal return already incorporated into you by all your training and all you had ever heard from your parents and your teachers. As the already always present thought becomes more and more conscious for you as you mature and begin to think about it, *then* the thought "would transform you as you are and perhaps crush you." The thought of eternal return is a *selecting* thought, a *separating* thought, depending on who you are. For some, the thought of eternal return transforms you, exalts you, gives you joy. For others, the thought of eternal return crushes you, depresses you, makes you despair. It all depends on what your disposition to life is; it depends on your love or hate of your own life.

That's all Nietzsche says about eternal return in this first public announcement of it in the second to last section of *Saint January*. Then comes the last section of *Saint January*. It pictures someone called "Zarathustra" leaving his home, going into the mountains, spending ten years there, and now preparing to return, ripe with a new teaching he had discovered in his solitude. And that ends *Saint January* and ends his book: dramatically, oddly, in a way that no reader could possibly understand and that every reader would find surprising and questionable. A few well-informed readers might know that Zarathustra was the great Persian prophet who was the founding teacher of transcendence and of an afterlife of reward for the good and punishment for the evil, but even they would wonder why Nietzsche ended his book on Zarathustra returning. Only Nietzsche knew what his reader could come to know only later, for the last section of *The Gay Science* is the first section of the book he was now planning to write, *Thus Spoke Zarathustra*, and that book would describe this great founding teacher preparing to return to humanity and eventually teaching eternal return. *Thus Spoke Zarathustra* exists to present the teaching of eternal return.

So the two great discoveries that Nietzsche wrote out in that notebook in the summer of 1881 set his writing career for the next years. The difference between those two discoveries can already be seen in Nietzsche's first public treatment of them in *The Gay Science*, where the ontology is a secret hidden at the center and eternal return is the prominent teaching announced at the end. And this way of presenting the two discoveries in *Saint January* set the pattern for how Nietzsche would treat them in *Thus Spoke Zarathustra* and in *Beyond Good and Evil*. *Saint January* set the pattern for understanding just what these two discoveries from Nietzsche's 1881 notebook are.

How the great books of Nietzsche's maturity treat his two great discoveries

In *Thus Spoke Zarathustra* the ontology of the drive to possess now bears the name *will to power*, and of course it appears first. *Will to power* is used once in Part 1, but as the peak insight into what lies behind "the greatest power on earth," morality. Only in Part 2 is will to power explained, but the explanation is for a limited and special audience only: those that he names "*you wisest.*" For them only, he names and explains will to power as the truth that lies behind their "will to truth." His explanation can come only after "The Dance Song," for there, in the poetry of that song, Zarathustra abandons his skeptical "Wild Wisdom," who had maintained that life or being is unfathomable, and he embraces instead his true love, Life herself, who suggests to him that she is *not unfathomable*. Life herself suggests to her lover Zarathustra that she can be *fathomed*, that she has a character or way that can be understood. Zarathustra then names and argues for "will to power" with "you wisest"; at the end of his argument he says to them, "Let us *talk* of this together"—they alone need to discuss with him his newly discovered and expressed ontological view.

Then Zarathustra ends his speech to the wisest saying, "There is many a house yet to be built." Will to power is a truth that needs to be known only by those with the most powerful passion to know—and they, together with Zarathustra, will build the house yet to be built; they will construct the teachings that will house future human beings, or be incorporated into future human beings. Eternal return is the new teaching, the *teaching for all* that will house future humanity. *Thus Spoke Zarathustra* therefore has eternal return appear only after Zarathustra has argued for will to power with the wisest: that is the necessary order for an *insight* for a few and a *teaching* for all.

Beyond Good and Evil treats will to power and eternal return in the same way. Nietzsche uses the phrase *will to power* four times in the first chapter on philosophy; will to power is what ultimately drives the highest inquiry, *philosophy*, and will to power drives all the things studied by *biology*, living things, and all the things studied by *physics*, all things, and the thing studied by *psychology*, the human soul. In that first chapter on philosophy Nietzsche gives no explanation of this fundamental truth; instead, as Strauss said, these all appear as *dogmatic* claims about will to power. In the next chapter, "The Free Mind," Nietzsche *does* offer an argument on behalf of will to power as the comprehensive truth, but his argument is only for his special audience of freed minds he has been educating. The ultimate step in their education is that well-prepared argument whose conclusion is that the world is will to power and nothing else. It's only for them, and we have already seen how even they react: "God is refuted but the devil is not." I will say more on that in my last lecture. As for eternal return, *Beyond Good and Evil* treats that in the *religion* chapter at just the right place in just the right way—as the public teaching for everyone, which arises out of the nihilism caused by the death of the old public teaching, the old religion.

So that's my main point: in the 1881 notebook Nietzsche became Nietzsche. There, he arrived for the first time at the two chief conclusions of his mature philosophy, first, an insight into the world as it is, the kind of insight that can interest only those whose ruling passion is the passion to know. And second, an insight into eternal return as the highest ideal of those whose natural disposition is to love life and love their own life. The first insight belongs to philosophy proper and the second belongs to philosophic poetry. What Nietzsche arrived at in the 1881 notebook determined the rest of his lifework, from *Saint January* through *Thus Spoke Zarathustra* and *Beyond Good and Evil* and on to the next major work that Nietzsche was planning and even writing when his breakdown occurred. In that last planned work too the will to power would be a *truth* to be thought through by those driven to think, whereas eternal return would be a *teaching* within which everyone could live their lives and celebrate their lives and celebrate the whole of life.

So the mature Nietzsche, the Nietzsche Nietzsche became, is a philosopher and a philosophic poet. In my final lecture I will say more about Nietzsche the philosophic poet. Here I want to end on one thing more about Nietzsche the philosopher: his relation to Plato. Nietzsche the philosopher achieves an ultimate ontological insight according to which to be is to be will to power and nothing else. Plato the philosopher achieves an ultimate ontological insight according to which to be is to be eros and nothing else. In my view these two insights are close kin, they are different ways of *wording* an insight that is similar. Here we are at the highest and hardest. Here the limitations of language and of thinking and of *my* thinking are most evident, but I want to try to summarize some of the aspects of the kinship of will to power and eros as ontologies.

Both assert the "*sovereignty of becoming*." Both assert that *becoming* is a surging and satisfying and surging again. Both assert that in that *ever-self-renewing activity* there is an internal directionality that aims at a kind of self-satisfaction: it is *auto-telic*. Both assert that this *discharging of energy or force* is a reaching beyond itself that encounters the *other* as a discharging of force reaching beyond *itself*, encounters the other as *resistance*. Both assert that this process of *directional energy- or force-expression* is *relational*; the relations are individual relations whose occurring is part of a field of such relations, where the total field of such relations is the *totality simply, all that is*.

Plato's language of *eros* is attractive and affirmative, expressing the process in human terms that make it easily lovable. Nietzsche's language of *will to power* is less attractive, in keeping with his tough-minded resolve to avoid what he called "word-tinsel" or verbal beautification, in favor of wording that described the process more exactly, though necessarily still inadequately, "as a weakening and limiting metaphor—as too human" (BGE 22). But those initial differences in the terms themselves mask what seems to me the fundamental kinship of understanding shared by Plato and Nietzsche.

Nietzsche became Nietzsche in a way similar to the way in which Socrates became Socrates. Genuine philosophers are genuine kin.

LECTURE 6

Nietzsche's Philosophic Poetry

I want to begin this last lecture with Strauss's formulation of proper method: "*The problem inherent in the surface of things and only in the surface of things is the heart of things.*" The surface of things to which he paid the most careful attention was the surface of philosophers' texts. There, woven into the surface through their art of writing, was the heart of things, what the philosopher who composed that surface wanted *you* to follow into the heart of things. And the heart of things that Strauss discovered and wanted his careful readers to discover was what a philosopher always aims to discover, the truth, ultimately the truth of being or of "what is"—the ontological truth. We can discover that truth only with the most responsible and thorough skeptical method that tests what is mere belief in order to discover if anything can be known. And Strauss showed that with good method, exegetical method that incorporates the philosophers' art of writing, we can read our way into the genuine heart of the philosophers Plato and Nietzsche. That heart is an ontology: to be is to be eros and nothing else, to be is to be will to power and nothing else. This main point of all my lectures leads to the second main point: genuine philosophy *generates* philosophic poetry, a teaching that can be lived. As Diotima put it in her description of the peak, philosophic *seeing* results in an *engendering* that is the making of poetry.

With that I arrive at today's topic: Nietzsche's philosophic poetry. In his essay on Nietzsche, Strauss looked first at Nietzsche's philosophy, even though the topic of his essay was religion in Nietzsche. In my second lecture we looked at what Strauss said about the most important section of *Beyond Good and Evil*, section 36, which contains the only argument for will to power in the book. I want to consider that argument again in order to see how it initiates the move to Nietzsche's philosophic poetry.

Nietzsche's philosophy: *Beyond Good and Evil* #36

Section 36 comes just after the center of "The Free Mind" chapter. The free mind had been Nietzsche's primary topic since he broke with Wagner and the Wagnerian perspective of his early books in August, 1876. Now, ten years later, the center of "The Free Mind" chapter deals with the conclusion that modern free minds have ultimately arrived at, "epistemological skepticism," skepticism that anything can really be *known*, the skepticism reinforced by Kant's account of knowing.

Nietzsche views this as the highest point reached by modern free minds, minds trained in their freedom partly by Nietzsche's books on the ideal of the free mind; these free minds represent his only possible audience, his "friends." In the long central section of the chapter, section 34, Nietzsche aims to raise a question about the finality of skepticism, about whether skepticism is in fact the highest attainment of the human intellect. Connected to that long section is the very short section 35, in which Nietzsche raises a powerful question about a hidden *motive* behind modern skepticism. Section 35 in its totality says this:

> O Voltaire! O humaneness! O nonsense! There is something about 'truth,' about the *search* for truth;

> when a human being goes about it too humanely—
> 'He seeks the true only to do the good'—I bet he finds
> nothing!

The French skeptic Voltaire had maintained that "*He seeks the true only to do the good*" (a statement Nietzsche wrote in French and that I translated into English). What is Nietzsche's point? It is an *accusation* against the skepticism of the free minds like Voltaire, who had been the hero of Nietzsche's first free mind book, *Human, All Too Human*. Nietzsche accuses the *search for the true* of modern free-minded skeptics of being fatally limited by their belief that the true and the good must coincide; their primary desire is to hold on to the modern *good*, to modern *virtue*, and that curbs their search for the true, making skepticism about knowledge an appealing fall-back position protecting their view of the good. Skepticism about knowledge excuses continued *belief* in modern virtue, allowing their unfree minds to hold on to the modern virtues of *equality of rights* and the *end of suffering*. In the classical language of the Voltaire quotation, belief about the *good* still binds their unfree minds, keeping them from the *true*. A search for the true as a support for their good is bound to fail: "I bet he finds nothing."

This lovely, humorous, profound accusation says that skepticism is attractive to modern, enlightened free minds because if you can't know the *true* then you can keep on believing in the *good*, the modern good. Skepticism gives permission to place morality above knowing. The epistemological skepticism of the *free minds* is really a sign of *bound minds*, minds that are merely moral.

So the two linked sections at the center of "The Free Mind" aim to provoke, to unsettle the free-minded reader in order to force a question on him about the actual freedom of his mind. And immediately after that challenge to his only possible audience, that invitation to perplexity, to doubt their doubt, Nietzsche makes his essential argument for what a truly free mind can know. It's clear: Nietzsche's careful placement of his only argument on behalf of the will to power view alerts his careful reader to the actual, historical setting for the ontological claim he is about to make: the times are unripe for such a claim, but the philosopher must nevertheless speak, he must voice his argument.

Nietzsche does not assume that his argument will be persuasive, however complete and valid it is. As a valid argument, what it does is *invite* the free minds to think about his argument, to question their skepticism and entertain the possibility of a fundamental truth that can be known. Nietzsche's strategy here is the same strategy his Zarathustra used: at the end of his only argument for will to power, Zarathustra says to his only audience "Let us *talk* of this, *you wisest.*" The audience for the argument in both of Nietzsche's most important books is the most select audience: *you wisest* in *Zarathustra*, *you freest minds* in *Beyond Good and Evil*; in both cases, only *you* need to concern yourself with this. This is the esoteric core of Nietzsche's thought, however much it lies open on the page.

Nietzsche's argument is subtle and has to be studied in all the steps he set out. Here I look only at the core of it, *look at it,* not explain its details or try to persuade you of anything. Remember, though, that Strauss praised it as "the most intransigent intellectual probity."

To open his argument, Nietzsche emphasizes that scientific method requires economy of principles and therefore: "we have to make the experiment of positing the causality of the will hypothetically as the only one," the only kind of cause. "*Have to*" because of the twofold demand of scientific method, *economy of principles* and that conclusions be drawn *hypothetically*. Therefore, "one has to risk the hypothesis . . . whether all mechanical occurrences are not, insofar as force is active in them, will force, effects of will." Wherever we recognize *cause* in nature we must suspend the view of classical modern physics (the physics of Descartes and Newton) that a *mechanics* of cause and effect is at work within a mechanistic world-whole. Instead we must view events in nature hypothetically as *will* events, events in which *will* is active.

Nietzsche then turns to *what* is to be investigated by this inquiry into cause. Having himself begun with what is given, *human passions and desires*, his subject for ten years, he here begins with his postulated basis for the instincts driving them: "Suppose we succeeded in explaining our entire instinctive life as the development and ramification of *one* basic form of the will—namely, of the will to power as *my* proposition has it." A free mind does what Nietzsche did, investigate one's self and other human beings to understand what the roots of all our actions may be. Beginning with knowledge of the human soul, can we explain our instinctual life as Nietzsche explained it, first as different forms of *Habsucht*, the addiction for having, the drive that he later came to understand more deeply as *will to power*. Suppose you *could* do that; then, in accord with good method, you must experimentally expand your conclusion about the roots of human action to a broader field: "suppose all organic functions could be traced back to this will to power." You must move from what explains human actions to an explanation of the functioning of all organic things, all living things, everything studied by the science of biology, the unstated premise that needs to be proven experimentally being that human beings are not essentially different from other living beings.

Finally, assuming you succeed in applying the hypothesis of will to power to the whole realm of living things: "then one would have gained the right to determine *all* efficient force univocally as—*will to power.* The world viewed from inside, the world defined and determined according to its 'intelligible character'—it would be 'will to power' and nothing else.—"

"Gained the right"—scientific method justifies, it even requires this broadest of all hypothetical expansions: explanatory success attainted with the human and the organic gives one the right to draw the broadest conclusion, the ontological conclusion first arrived at in the 1881 notebook, then merely hinted at as the secret of what I share with the waves in Nietzsche's first ever public presentation of it, and what Zarathustra then shared with *you wisest* in *Thus Spoke Zarathustra.*

In *Beyond Good and Evil* Nietzsche leaves it at that. He stops there. He has made his argument and you, with your free mind, are to think whether the conclusion can be cogent and true or not. Nietzsche put a little dash at the end of this section 36, and this little punctuation mark suggests a connection with the very short section 37: as Strauss noted, sections 36 and 37 resemble in form the pair of sections Nietzsche placed at the center, 34 and 35. By making 36 and 37 a pair, Nietzsche moves from *philosophy* to *philosophic poetry.*

Nietzsche's move from philosophy to philosophic poetry: BGE section 37

Section 37 is a *response,* an immediate reaction by Nietzsche's audience to his conclusion that the world is will to power and nothing else. In section 37 Nietzsche allows his true audience of free minds to speak up immediately and say what *they* think, how they *feel* about the conclusion they have just heard: "What? Doesn't this mean, to speak in the popular way: God is refuted but the devil is not—?" The free minds are *shocked*. They confirm what Nietzsche suggested of modern free minds in section 35: they are not fully free but are bound by their view of the coincidence of the true and the good; if will to power is true, their good of perpetual peace at the end of history in a paradise of equality of rights and the end of suffering is neither attainable nor true. Nietzsche says they speak in "the popular way": they adopt the common language of God and devil. But they are the free minds: they don't believe in God or the devil. They speak in the popular way because only that language can express their extreme feeling. Only the old extremes of God and devil can express the horror they feel about his reasoned will to power conclusion.

Put into less theological language, their reaction says that if the world is "will to power and nothing else," then everything they hold high and noble and good is destroyed and replaced by what seems to them low and ignoble and evil. Your conclusion that everything is a conflict of drives for power is a horrifying, ugly, evil view. Isn't *that* what your will to power view means? "On the contrary! On the contrary, my friends!" Nietzsche's response is as emphatic as theirs, but it needs an explanation he does not give. *You* have to think the contrary, and it is easily stated in the popular language the free minds just used: *The devil is refuted but God is not.* As Strauss says five times, Nietzsche's view is "a vindication of God."

Nietzsche's words, "On the contrary! On the contrary!," carry a deep theological lesson for his friends, modern free minds who have lost interest in theology and lost any sense of why religion is important. His contrary says: there is something seriously wrong with your concept of God and devil. Just reverse them and you get closer to the truth. And that reversal succeeds in denouncing the only theology they can imagine, Christian theology. "On the contrary! On the contrary!" implies this: Your concept of God (which of course they do not believe in), a transcendent, supernatural Being who created the world, watches the world, judges the world—think of that as the devil. And your concept of the devil (which they believe in even less), the Lord of this world, the *Prince of Darkness*, as Christian theology calls him, taking the whole world as fallen and belonging to the devil—think of *that* as divine. *What is a god?*—that is what Nietzsche makes his free-minded atheist friends ask.

Nietzsche has a final theological instruction: "And as to the devil, who forces you to speak in the popular way!—" *Who?* The old God forces them, the God who is dead but not gone, the moral God whose concept still rules their view of what a god is. You have a lot to learn theologically, Nietzsche suggests to his free-minded friends, us modern atheists. Nietzsche asked, who forces you to speak of the devil? He did not ask, who forces you *to speak of God*. And he did not ask because speaking of God is what Nietzsche wants: a new way of saying what a god is or what the gods are.

So, what just happened in Nietzsche's book? Just after the center of his second chapter on philosophy, the chapter on "The Free Mind," Nietzsche placed his only philosophical argument for the will to power in *Beyond Good and Evil*. It is an argument of "the most intransigent intellectual probity" and leads to a comprehensive conclusion about the being of beings. Then, immediately, he hears his friends link that philosophical conclusion to religion: his only possible audience reacts in religious terms. And what does Nietzsche do? He *stays* with religion while suggesting that, no, his philosophic view does not refute God but vindicates God properly understood.

In his religion chapter Nietzsche will describe his audience of modern free minds this way: "they no longer even know what religions are good for" (BGE 58). Nietzsche knows what religions are good for and he deals with that in the final two sections of his religion chapter. Those sections argue that religions are good for, necessary for, any social order. Religion, taught to the young, *incorporated* into the young, gives guidance to what is good and bad, noble and base, what is worth living for and what it is necessary to reject. These sections show the uses of religion in binding the rulers to the ruled, offering others a disciplined path to higher spirituality, and making life endurable for the common people. For religion to be *healthy*, Nietzsche argues in these sections, it must be guided in the appropriate way by wise men, by philosophers, by those not themselves guided by religion. Philosophy must rule religion; reason must rule the instinct to worship and adore.

Nietzsche views religion as necessary and desirable. More than that, he can speak of the "god-creating instinct" in human beings and say in amazement, "almost two thousand years and not a single new god!" (A 19). He is not really amazed because he knows the reason: the last two thousand years in the West have been ruled by the jealous God, the God of monotheism, the God whose jealousy gave Nietzsche his best joke: "One of the gods said one day, 'There is only one God, thou shalt have no other gods before me.' And all the other gods—died laughing. Thus there was only one God."

In his religion chapter, while criticizing Christianity, Nietzsche looked back to the polytheistic religion of the ancient Greeks, Homeric religion, and praised it for "the enormous abundance of gratitude it displays." The problem is not gods as such, the problem is the God of Revelation, the God of Christianity from whom modern minds have freed themselves, and made tremendous gains in free thinking. But also, and this is Nietzsche's point here, those gains have come at tremendous cost, the cost of gods as such, the cost of no longer even knowing what religions are good for.

Nietzsche knows what religions are good for; philosophers know what religions are good for, as Socrates showed in Plato's *Republic* when he altered or reformed Homeric religion in the time of its dying for intelligent young men. Only religion can structure the daily life of a culture; cultures live on beliefs and practices, on incorporated beliefs that one takes in from the earliest age in the stories told to little children and reinforces in the rituals and festivals and customs that give meaning and structure to ordinary daily life. And for religion to be viable, Nietzsche seems to think, there must be gods. I will speak about the actual gods to whom Nietzsche points later. But first, having seen from sections 36 and 37 how religion or philosophic poetry arises naturally out of Nietzsche's philosophy, I want to look briefly at the aspect of Nietzsche's philosophic poetry that Nietzsche put first in *Beyond Good and Evil*, before speaking of gods at its very end.

Philosophic poetry 1: eternal return

Instead of making God or gods the main theme of his religion chapter in *Beyond Good and Evil*, Nietzsche made its theme roughly the history of Western religion, of Christianity. And he placed at the very center of his religion chapter the crisis of Western religion. That crisis is a religious catastrophe with two aspects: *the death of God* and what he calls *the assassination of the old soul concept*. Just after these central sections Nietzsche placed the completely understandable next step, the step into the deepest catastrophe: nihilism, the growing sense among modern free minds that nothing is truly of worth. Then, just after that, with his historical sketch complete into the present moment, Nietzsche put the only section in *Beyond Good and Evil* to deal with eternal return. In that section, 56, a philosopher sees the affirmation of eternal return arising as a future possibility out of the nihilism that results from the death of God and the assassination of the old soul concept. I touched on Strauss's use of section 56 in my second Strauss lecture, but I want to look at it more closely here as my first main point on Nietzsche's philosophic poetry.

Nietzsche ended his section on nihilism saying, "We all already know something of this.—" That dash at the end of that statement leads to the next section, which begins: "Whoever has endeavored with some enigmatic longing, as I have, to think pessimism to its depths . . . whoever has really . . . looked into, down into the most world-denying of all possible ways of thinking." "[*A*]*s I have*"—the whole section will be about Nietzsche the thinker driven to think modern pessimism to its depth. That "enigmatic longing" driving him can only be philosophy; the philosopher today is driven to investigate "the most world-denying of all possible ways of thinking."

Nietzsche goes on to identify himself further: he stands "beyond good and evil and no longer . . . under the spell and delusion of morality." Driven to free himself of the prejudices of morality, the philosopher Nietzsche "may just thereby, without really meaning to do so, have opened his eyes to the opposite ideal: the ideal of the most high-spirited, alive, world-affirming human being."

Nietzsche the thinker moves from thinking through one ideal, the most world-*denying* possible way of thinking, to "the opposite ideal," which is the most world-*affirming* possible way of thinking. I want to emphasize what Strauss emphasized: the little clause that Nietzsche put in here, "without really meaning to do so." Those words are important because of what they say about Nietzsche's intention: he did not undertake his investigation in order to discover a new ideal. He is not driven by a need for a new morality or a new religion; instead, he is driven by the "enigmatic longing" that is the need to understand—he is a philosopher and not a moralist and not a religious man.

The new ideal he glimpses without really meaning to do so is "the ideal of the most high-spirited, alive, world-affirming human being . . . who wants to have *what was and is* repeated into all eternity, shouting insatiably *da capo* (from the beginning)." That person, the most world-affirming human being, wants the eternal return of the world, *wants* it. Eternal return is his ideal, eternal return is what is desired by the most world-affirming human being. And Nietzsche immediately clarifies that wanting: "not only to himself but to the whole play and spectacle, and not only to a spectacle but at bottom to him who needs precisely this spectacle. . . ." The affirmation of the whole spectacle is ultimately the self-affirmation of the human spectator on the spectacle—the affirmation is an affirmation of the world because the world makes the philosopher possible, because the world generated a spectator who is a rational, self-conscious, knowing fragment of the knowable whole.

That is all that *Beyond Good and Evil* says about eternal return. But it is enough for a book whose intention it is to be "a critique of modernity." In its critique of modern religion it provides, with great brevity and great precision, a pointer to what could lie beyond the nihilism in which modernity's needed demolition of Christianity left religion as a whole for enlightened Western moderns. Eternal return, then, is part of Nietzsche's philosophic poetry, the new highest ideal; it is what ideals necessarily are, a positing by a human being, the valuing being, of the highest ideal. And with that summary, I move to a second aspect of Nietzsche's philosophic poetry that Nietzsche, again consistently, only pointed to in *Beyond Good and Evil*, that book of critique.

Philosophic poetry 2: gods

When Strauss discussed Nietzsche's religion chapter in *Beyond Good and Evil* he got to a certain point and said, "There is an important ingredient, not to say the nerve, of Nietzsche's 'theology' of which I have not spoken and shall not speak." With this emphatic, this vehement refusal Strauss avoids speaking about the *nerve* of Nietzsche's theology that seems to be his introduction of gods. Strauss had suggested that Nietzsche "had doubts whether there can be a world, any world whose center is not God," and *world* here means *cultural* world, the world inhabited by human beings, believing beings. Strauss, a philosopher who is a Jew and who had a lifelong sensitivity to the fate of Judaism in the twentieth century, refuses to speak about the theological-political project that Nietzsche suggested could be the center of a future world. But Nietzsche himself *must* speak, precisely because there cannot be a "world whose center is not God." And Nietzsche knew that he had a problem in speaking about gods because his only possible audience were the modern free-minded skeptics who "no longer even know what religions are good for" and for whom the only imaginable God was the dead God of monotheism they are only too happy to help kill off.

Nietzsche said "I rarely speak as a theologian," but he exaggerated. However unwelcoming the times were, he had to speak as a theologian in order to introduce a new concept of what a god is to those who had incorporated the old concept of God. He began to speak as a theologian in *Beyond Good and Evil* section 37 when he suggested that the devil was refuted but God was not. And he suggested in the appropriate places in his book that religion and gods were indispensable. But he saved his actual view of what a god is until the last possible moment: he placed a first taste of his new teaching about the gods prominently, at the very end, and he expressed his view in the most beautiful section of the book, section 295. There, finally, Nietzsche spoke as a theologian.

He began with a long, lovely description of his experience with "the tempter god" that Strauss called "a super-Socrates." Nietzsche describes him hauntingly, magnetically, but does not name him. When he finally gets around to naming him, he says he is "no less a one than the god, Dionysos, that great ambiguous one and tempter god to whom I once offered . . . my first-born." Nietzsche's "first-born" is his first book, *The Birth of Tragedy*, where Dionysos is described as the forceful, ecstatic god behind Greek tragedy.

> Meanwhile I have learned much . . . more about the philosophy of this god . . . I the last disciple and initiate of the god Dionysos—and I suppose that I might begin at long last to offer you, my friends, a few tastes of this philosophy. . . .

Nietzsche has learned a lot about Dionysos since his first book, enough to think of himself as "the last disciple and initiate" of this god. He has also learned a lot about his audience, those to whom he must now speak about the gods. His view that the gods philosophize will offend philosophers, he says, because they have all been "on the same track" theologically since Plato and Plato's Diotima taught that the gods do not philosophize because they are already wise—the *philosophers* will oppose a philosopher introducing a concept of philosophizing gods. But what about his friends? "Among you, my friends, it will not seem so offensive, unless it comes too late and not at the right moment; for today, as I have been told, you no longer like to believe in God and gods. Perhaps I shall have to carry my frankness further in my tale than will always be pleasing to the strict habits of your ears?"

What Nietzsche has to say about gods will also offend his friends, but offend them for a different reason: it comes *at the wrong time* for them. His friends are not yet ready to hear any talk of gods because it is too soon after their liberation from the old God—Nietzsche's friends, newly liberated atheists, do not want to hear anything about gods because of their recent release from the tyrannical God. But Nietzsche must speak of gods and can only speak in the present, however too soon the present is.

Among the theological lessons Nietzsche dares to speak to his friends is a very important one that belongs to the *much* that he has learned since *The Birth of Tragedy*: the god Dionysos is always accompanied by another god, his beloved, *Ariadne*. Dionysos and Ariadne. Those are the two gods Nietzsche introduces. Why does Nietzsche, who knows what gods are good for, introduce *these* two gods and *only* these two? Of course, he does not believe that humanity could go backward and reestablish the religion of Homer, who first named these two gods. What makes these two gods different and worthy of being reintroduced in late modern times?

As Strauss noted, Nietzsche thought that human beings had a "god-making instinct," a natural inclination in us to make into gods what we hold highest. It belongs to our nature to *divinize*, to make into divine persons whatever it is that we most honor. And what do we most honor or hold highest if what we desire is the eternal return of life? We hold life itself highest. And life is the constantly renewing cycle of being born and dying, being born through sexual reproduction and dying. Dionysos and Ariadne are sexual reproduction elevated by the god-making instinct into gods; they are sexual reproduction divinized. Dionysos is the god of *maleness or manliness*. Ariadne is the god of *femaleness or womanliness*. Dionysos and Ariadne are a *pair*, the productive, generative pair of all life. As a pair, they belong together in their difference; they are the war between the sexes and the love between the sexes. That is the specialness, the singularity of the divine pair; Dionysos and Ariadne are life on earth, its being born and dying, raised to the highest elevation of honor that humans can confer. Dionysos and Ariadne are the universal gods of earthly reproduction given local or Greek names. And they are so much more, but I will mention only one other point: Dionysos is a philosophizing god—he is driven to understand. And Ariadne? She does not philosophize; in some more fundamental sense she already knows, *she* has the thread that leads out of the mystery at the heart of the labyrinth, as the Greek myth of Ariadne held.

So, of course, Nietzsche as a theologian singled out these two gods as the gods of the earthly religion intimately connected with the affirmation of the eternal return of life. But with these divinities we see immediately that Nietzsche the theologian could not do what Plato the theologian could do when *he* introduced new, non-Homeric gods: Socrates says in the *Republic* that he can leave the practices and rituals, the song and dance, to the already established institutions. These already established or incorporated practices and rituals will adapt to the new. Part of Nietzsche's problem is that there are no established institutions honoring Dionysos and Ariadne. Nietzsche's problem with introducing new gods is the same problem he had introducing a new highest ideal: How to *incorporate* a new sense of what a god is and how to generate the festivals, the song and dance, that celebrate new gods. Gods too seem believable only when they have always already been believed, when they are the gods of the ancestors that we have known since childhood, and when we already know how to sing their praises and how to dance our gratitude.

I must also note that Nietzsche said in his autobiography, "There is nothing in me of the founder of a religion" (*Ecce Homo* 4.1). Nietzsche the philosopher tempts prospective knowers, not prospective believers, however few the knowers are, however many the believers are, and however much the knowers know that only around a god can everything turn into "world." With respect to gods it seems that Nietzsche says this to his friends: *recognize* the necessity of religion; *recognize* the universal naturalness of Dionysos and Ariadne as the gods of life: *recognize* that and leave it to the god-making instinct. The love of life will do what love does in human beings, prompt us to divinize, to make divine what we most love, life as reproduced through sexuality. Dionysos and Ariadne are the natural gods of human beings in love with life and the natural human instinct to make gods will see to their rebirth.

There is a third aspect of Nietzsche's philosophic poetry that has not been widely recognized. And I want to end on that because it seems to me particularly promising.

Philosophic poetry 3: ecology; the human way of being on the earth

Like eternal return and the gods Dionysos and Ariadne, this third matter springs from Nietzsche's *philosophy*, his understanding of the human as a form of life on earth that is connected with and dependent upon the whole network of life that evolved it. This philosophic view of human life on earth generates principles of human action whose basic imperative is the one that Nietzsche's Zarathustra gave first when he returned from the mountains: "*Be true to the earth!*" Nietzsche is the first Western philosopher to teach a comprehensive ecological philosophy; his is a comprehensive moral and political teaching based fundamentally on love of the earth, where the earth is understood as the *this-worldly* as opposed to some beyond, as the *temporal* as opposed to any timeless transcendence, as the *always mortal* as opposed to any immortality—and as *will to power* and nothing else.

This third aspect of Nietzsche's philosophic poetry, ecology, love of life on earth, has an advantage over the first two aspects: both a highest ideal and gods must be *incorporated*; they seem to be possible or effective only if they are *already* believed, *already* tradition. But the contrary ideal and God are the now-already incorporated, and they still exercise power even over those who have come to doubt or disbelieve them. Consequently, we can hardly imagine a wholly different ideal or wholly different gods. Finally, skeptical modern doubters like ourselves have a *prejudice* against all high ideals and gods, which may be the strongest resistance to a Nietzschean poetry that employs them.

But this third aspect of Nietzsche's political philosophy, an ethics of ecology or environmentalism, is something that could be much more easily welcomed by a contemporary audience, by us. Instead of being repelled by it, we are drawn to it from the start. This has been part of my understanding of Nietzsche's philosophic politics since my first book, *Nietzsche's Teaching*. In my second book, *Nietzsche and Modern Times*, I described Nietzsche as the comprehensive ecological philosopher. Since writing those books I have come to see how very helpful Leo Strauss is on this point of Nietzsche's political philosophy. In my second Strauss lecture I read Strauss's words from paragraph 35 of his Nietzsche essay. They express Strauss's main point about the complementary man:

> His supremacy is shown by the fact that he solves the highest, most difficult problem.

Strauss defines that problem: "man is conquering nature and there are no assignable limits to that conquest." To solve the highest problem of modern times is to find good grounds for assigning limits to the conquest of nature. I don't find in Strauss any general ecological or environmental interest of the sort that has by now become popular and significant. Instead, Strauss warns against the conquest of nature as the conquest of *human* nature through the modern ideals of equality of rights and the end of suffering. That modern conquest of human nature would mean the end of philosophy on earth, because philosophy depends upon the recognition and encouragement of an order of rank and the continuation of suffering properly understood, understood as the human struggle to attain the high, most especially knowledge; *that* known suffering from a lack can be remedied only through sacrificial struggle—subordination of every drive to the drive for knowledge. Strauss made that the culmination of his Nietzsche essay, the high end-point, Strauss at his most relevant. The modern threat to the human greatness that is philosophy can be *solved* by Nietzsche's theological-political program, his ministerial poetry, because it assigns limits to the modern conquest of nature out of the love of nature, a love expressed in the highest ideal that the whole of nature return just as it is an infinite number of times.

I want to end my lectures on that theme by looking at Nietzsche's own first *coming to* that solution to the most difficult problem, Nietzsche's first full insight into this greatest of late-modern practical problems and its solution. I have emphasized that Nietzsche's comprehensive philosophic view first came together, first gained completeness, in his 1881 notebook, the notebook in which both the ontology of what became will to power and the affirmation of eternal return appear for the first time. That notebook also contains what as far as I know is Nietzsche's first statement of this ecological or environmentalist aspect of his philosophic poetry. And remember, Nietzsche wrote the 1881 notebook before "*Saint January*," the fourth Part of *The Gay Science*, before *Thus Spoke Zarathustra*, and before *Beyond Good and Evil*.

The entry I want to discuss appears early in that notebook. Because of the specific problems that had occupied Nietzsche in the writing of *Daybreak*, this early entry in the notebook that he began after finishing *Daybreak* begins on the theme of most of the early entries, his ongoing reflection on morality, more specifically on his insight that the moral distinction between egoism and altruism hides the fact that all human actions are fundamentally egoistic, or serve the *I*. This entry falls among the entries that expand the field of that egoism as *Habsucht*, the drive to possess, and that Nietzsche will soon expand to an ontology or a true account of the nature of all beings.

The entry (numbered 11 [21] Frühjahr-Herbst 1881 in the Colli-Montinari *Kritische Gesamtausgabe*) opens by setting out the task: "To describe the history of the *I-feeling*: and to show that in altruism too this wanting to possess is the essential matter." Nietzsche's "history of the I-feeling" therefore begins with what underlies morality. *Wanting to possess*, the *drive to have*, the essential matter in the *I-feeling*, is basic to both egoism and altruism, the feeling for the other that has been misunderstood as the opposite of egoism. The rest of the entry describes what the *history* of the I-feeling could become; it moves out beyond the exclusiveness of *egoism* and out beyond the feeling of *altruism* to broader fields beyond the I and the other. The rest of the entry looks like a sketch for a book about what Nietzsche is discovering and writing out in this notebook regarding the drive to possess, first discovered as the truth about egoism.

The entry goes on: "To show how the chief progress in morality does not lie in the concept 'Not-I and I' but instead in the sharper understanding of the *true* in the other, in me, and in nature." So the issue is a sharper understanding of what is *true* of both the I and the other—and then that great expansion, to *nature*. That word is especially important because it extends the need for a sharper understanding to *nature itself*, to the *nature of nature*, the nature that is of course also present in the other [person] and in me.

What that sharper understanding allows the knower to do comes next: "thus to free *wanting to possess* more and more from the mere appearance of possession, from *fabricated* possession, and therefore to purify the I-feeling from self-deception." The German word for *fabricated* or *made* is *erdichteten*, which can be understood literally as *poetized*. But the important thing here is this: *the chief progress* in morality is to gain a sharper understanding of what the genuine drive to possession really is: the chief progress in morality is coming *to know* what is true about the drive to possess; and that knowing *purifies* the I-feeling, freeing it from illusion or self-deception.

Nietzsche then describes what that sharper understanding of the true in the I and the other and nature may actually be, what the purifying of the I-feeling from self-deception would make possible: "Perhaps it ends in this: that instead of the I, we recognize the relatedness and the enemy-ness of things." The "perhaps" must be noticed. Nietzsche is looking ahead *wondering*, will this process end where it actually did end, in the *knowing* in which it actually ended? Attempting to purify the I from self-deception may *culminate in recognizing* that all things are *related* in *what they are*, related but in a relatedness that includes "enemy-ness." It may end in a unitary *kinship* and *enmity*, likeness and strife. Here we can hear the beginning of the will to power view.

The error of the I, its self-deception, would thus be its sense of itself as something wholly distinct from the other, and the engine of progress in morality could not lie in the concept "Not I and I" because that very concept is deceptive. It masks what is fundamental; it obscures the common source of the Not I and the I that lies in the dynamic impersonal process that generates both the *I-feeling* and its sense of the other, its altruistic sense. That process is a relatedness and enemy-ness which extends beyond the I and not-I to the *true* in *nature* itself.

The entry on the I-feeling then moves to what seems to be a first consequence of recognizing the relatedness/enemy-ness of things: "To live not 'for the sake of the other' but 'for the sake of the true!'" This sentence is the first of a sequence of eleven sentences each ending with an exclamation mark, a punctuation mark that heightens the importance of each statement with a sense of resolve. This first such sentence states what *not* to live for, *the other*, what both Christian ethics and its successor modern ethics demand; it seems to herald a fundamental shift in what the social order is to live for—for the sake of the true.

Living "for the sake of the true," Nietzsche says, would "Reshape the I-feeling! Weaken the personal tendency! Habituate the eye to the reality of things!" These short sentences, each with its exclamation mark, serve to partially define what this move away from the dominant ethics would gain: a reshaping of the I-feeling would weaken the personal tendency, allow the impersonal to dominate, and habituate one to the genuine reality of things that underlies I, you, and nature. The imperatives point to the felt need to *do* the things said: *reshape, weaken, habituate*. The short sentences continue in sentences that I omit; each has its exclamation mark and all lead up to a last sentence of the same kind: "There's something new to create: not I, not you, and not all!" The new that is not I, you, or all would see the "relatedness and enemyness of the things" in the I, you, and all. Beginning with seeing the I-feeling in a new way would lead to seeing *you* and the *whole* in a new way that marks progress in morality by aligning it with the true.

So the entry gives a sketch of the future stages in the *history of the I-feeling* leading up to this final stage of seeing that there is something new to create. Nietzsche, the solitary thinker, anticipates those stages. He is the philosopher whose progress in thinking, whose understanding of those stages led him to see the need to create something new that is not I as I was, or you as you were, nor the all as it was. And if it is in fact a sketch for a book, then the purpose of the book would be to lead its reader to think those stages of understanding and to see this need to create something new.

This is half the notebook entry. I want to say something general about that first half before moving to the second half. Despite what might seem to be the case in this statement about "progress in morality," Nietzsche is not a utopian: he doesn't dream of some imaginary perfect outcome at the end of the history of the I-feeling, as moderns typically do, some perfect end of history. Nietzsche explicitly and reasonably claims not to be a utopian, not a dreamer, and the notebook makes clear why he is right in that claim: he has understood the process that made humans what we are, the molding process of history and culture that is based on the real drives that constitute us. We humans are always already made by our incorporation of a particular balance of the drives, our incorporation of a particular cultural teaching on good and bad that organizes the drives, judges their goodness and badness, and puts them into an order of rank. That incorporated cultural balance is always a tension, always an uneasy hierarchical resolution of the fundamental impulses and drives. Humans will always be *the uneasy beings*, living the particular forms of suffering that our particular psychic and social orders of rank impose on us. The promise of Nietzsche's teaching is not some utopia; instead, its promise is that out of the nihilism and turmoil at the end of the moral period can come a better reorganization of the drives, better because it fosters stronger and more noble specimens of the human species, better because healthier for that reason. And that whole shift in moral acting is based on one thing only, a philosopher's better understanding of the passions and a better disposition toward them, a better understanding and appreciation of the I-feeling and what it shares with the other and with nature.

Now we can turn to the new paragraph that ends the entry in the notebook. It is marked at the start by an "NB"—those two letters that in Latin stand for "Note Well." And this NB marks an *extremely* important NB: "NB. No *possession* in the young to strive *to must have (müssen) or to want (wollen)*!: as well as no *prestige* for command over others—these two drives are *not to be developed* at all!" I translate Nietzsche's German here completely literally into awkward English, not very grammatical English, because it is necessary to be exact. *Striving (erstreben)* is simply given, it's what we do as humans: striving is basic to the drives—drives always strive for *something*. The basic striving can be developed or encouraged to strive in *this* direction and not to strive in *that* direction. That is what *enculturation* does, what education or incorporation does: train us to strive in some particular direction. That's what Nietzsche's NB is for: his *new program of incorporation* aims to create "something new"—to redirect *striving* in order to foster and encourage the new I-feeling, leading to the new feeling for the *you* and for the *all*. The most basic training of the young is now to be informed by Nietzsche's insight into the history of the *I-feeling*.

The first step in that new training is what *not* to train for: first, *not* for any *possession*—just what that can mean Nietzsche will explain next. And *not* for the *prestige* of command over others. The German word I translate as *prestige* is *Ansehen*, which means here *to be seen as something special*. No *singling out* of the I then, in *command* over others. This is a philosopher speaking, a solitary thinker who with the greatest intellectual and spiritual effort arrived at a new understanding of the I-feeling, and now he speaks as an educator: how can his new understanding be trained into others? These *others* are not the few like him: those few he can tempt or teach to think their way out of the old understanding. Instead, he here speaks of the education or training from youth up in society as a whole: because *some* total view is always incorporated into all the young, Nietzsche looks to the new view that is to be incorporated.

After what *not* to train into the young, the paragraph marked by NB treats what the young *are* to be taught. Here we come to the most important matter. NB the positive content of the new education, what it aims to train in: "*Letting* us *be possessed* by the things (not by persons) and by the largest possible range of *true things*."

Instead of teaching the young to strive to want possession and thereby develop in themselves the old I-feeling, and instead of teaching the young to feel prestige by commanding others, teach the young what the philosopher himself had learned in the first paragraph. *He* had learned to free himself from the false I-feeling of a separated, isolated, possessive I and had won the freedom to know the relatedness of all things, and that *knowing* led him to experience the desire to be taken over by the true things, the desire to let the true things *be the things they are* in him, too. That experience in knowing by the philosophic knower—an experience that culminated in knowing what is to be will to power and nothing else—led him to his NB, his task to educate the young in the new stage in the history of the I-feeling that he is the first to experience, the experience in which the *I-feeling* is to let things be the true things they are, to want the natural things to be what they are in their continuous becoming and decaying, in their natural order of rank, and in all the other facets of their naturalness. The two separate paragraphs of this notebook entry show Nietzsche repeating what genuine philosophers experience: their insight into *what is* is followed by insight into the action necessary in their present on behalf of that insight. In the second part of this notebook entry, therefore, Nietzsche moves to ministerial poetry, to the teaching that can structure the social order anew by being trained into the young. Here are the beginnings of the future content of Nietzsche's ministerial poetry. And it begins with incorporation, training in the new, true, I-feeling in its exposure to the true things.

Nietzsche's history of the I-feeling needs one final step. Having just spoken of being possessed "by the largest possible range of *true things*," he says: "What *grows* out of that can be anticipated: we become *farmland* for the things." Nietzsche can easily predict what grows out of being possessed by the true things because he knows what we humans are: *Ackerland* in German, *farmland, arable soil, productive earth* out of which particular "plants" naturally grow and flourish. It's easy to know what comes after being taken over by the true things because it *grows* out of us as plants grow out of fruitful soil. The last step in the history of the I-feeling describes what these "plants" are that grown naturally out of the fruitful soil of those who have incorporated the true things:

> *Images of existence* will grow out of us: and we would then be as this fruitfulness compels us to be: our inclinations/disinclinations are those of the farmland that would bring forth such fruit.

Letting the true things be what they are generates from our productive soil *new* images of existence that spring forth in accord with our inclinations and disinclinations as beings whose *natural* character it is to be productive of images. Now, our *learned* incorporated character produces images that celebrate and let be what naturally is in its coming to be and passing away.

"*Images of existence.*" That is the last step in Nietzsche's history of the I-feeling. We human beings are, by nature, *making* beings, *creating* beings. Here we touch Plato again, who could make this point easily with Greek vocabulary. In his *Symposium* Plato used the word *poiein*, which means in its most general sense *to make*: we human beings are the making beings; and in a particular sense *poiein* means to make poetry: we human beings are the poetizing beings. Humans are the making beings who make poetry by nature: words and songs spring out of us by nature, generated by our fruitful soil. So here, where *images of existence* are the subject, Nietzsche and

Plato unite in the fundamental way. Generated in us by our inclinations and disinclinations, by our *loves* and *hates*, are the images of existence that we live by, images that come to have authority for us as pictures or ideas of the worthy and the unworthy. The images of existence that humans generate become the standards of *how to be* and *what to be*, what to strive for and what to strive against. Nietzsche's history of the I-feeling anticipates new images of existence that accord with the true things now understood. Nietzsche ends where a philosopher always ends, with philosophy's *poetry*, within which humans will dwell on the earth. The new images of existence conceptualize the earth as the natural home of humanity; biological science studies the interconnected web of life on the planet; political and social movements make ecology central to decision-making or, as Strauss words it, assign limits to the conquest of nature out of love of nature.

Nietzsche adds one last sentence: "These images of existence are *the most important* that there have been till now: they will rule over humanity."

Nietzsche ends where Plato ends: Philosophers come to know that humanity is ruled by images, images incorporated into the young and exercising their rule over us in our maturity. Knowing the rule of images and compelled by the interests of philosophy to rule, philosophers rule by legislating the images. Plato ruled through images of transcendence: the ideas, the reformed Homeric gods, the immortal soul, a rewarding and punishing Hades. Plato's images succeeded because they serve deep drives that are part of the human make-up. Nietzsche's new images of existence aim to rule over humanity as Plato's images ruled over humanity but are now dying and deserve to die. Nietzsche's images have a promise of success because they too serve deep drives that are part of the human make-up, affirmative drives in conflict with the drives that Nietzsche saw as the drives that Plato's images of transcendence came to serve, negating drives of hatred and vengeance.

Nietzsche's new images of existence are what we have already seen as key elements of Nietzsche's philosophic poetry: the image of the *highest ideal*, what Plato called the Good that rules over all things in its transcendent fixity like the sun—a wholly imaginary sun in Plato, forever the same and giving existence to the ideas that are forever the same. Nietzsche's new highest ideal is not an eternal fixity but the eternal return of ever-changing life just as it is. And the image of particular *highest beings*, beings that "the god-creating instinct" generates in the making beings. In Plato, the highest beings tend toward the monotheism of the Good, while the platonic gods are moral judges who reward and punish us now and in the afterlife. The god-making instinct of our fruitful farmland can replace those now unbelievable and unworthy gods by new highest beings. (And I want to mention again the historic events in Western philosophy that lie behind Nietzsche's *blame* of Plato: platonism prepared the way for the rule of Christianity in Rome; that "platonism for the people" prepared the necessary modern war against it; but European modernity carried forward secular versions of Christian virtues, the modern ideals of the end of suffering and equality of rights; and it is those late consequences of platonism that Nietzsche acts to supplant—"letting be" in Nietzsche's sense carries no suggestion that unnatural ideals should be allowed to be what they are; his "letting be" knows the necessity of warfare on its behalf.) Nietzsche gave his images of the highest beings the already existing Greek names of Dionysos and Ariadne. These gods are not our judges; they don't punish or reward us; we don't have to bow down to them or beg them for favors. Instead, they are like us in being like what all life is, male and female, sexual, generative beings far superior to us in their manliness and womanliness. They are worthy of being emulated or copied by us, as far as we are able. We look up to them, they lift us up by being what they are. They are what we would most dearly love to be like.

Nietzsche's images of existence take these two particular forms of a highest ideal and of the highest beings. He has other images of existence, a new good and bad, for instance, capable of judging by natural, affirmative standards, but we can summarize them all as in the service of the fundamental passion of attraction, the passion of love.

That's Nietzsche's whole story, told early as the history of the I-feeling. His story ends in the human love of the earth as it naturally is and a love of the human as it naturally is, or as it can be, beyond the rule of images of existence that teach unnatural ideals wreaking vengeance on life as it is. His whole story ends in *ecology*, in knowledge of the interconnectedness of life on earth that generates the human imperative to be true to the earth. That's why it makes sense to me to see Nietzsche as the first comprehensive ecological philosopher. And that aspect of Nietzsche's philosophic poetry seems to me to be a *promising way* of entering Nietzsche, by seeing him as the founding thinker of an already popular movement that appeals to late modern people. That ecological movement, already strong in certain parts of the West, is bound to get stronger as the evidence becomes ever more undeniable that environmental disasters are caused by human-initiated climate change. Such movements, springing up from particular concerns, find their natural philosopher in Nietzsche.

This ecological aspect of Nietzsche' philosophic poetry has a kind of priority for me because of how it stands, or could stand, to the first two aspects of Nietzsche's philosophic poetry, eternal return, and earthly gods. The new images of existence, finding their start in Nietzsche's view of the ecological interrelatedness of nature, life, and human life on this planet, could eventually lead to new gods true to the earth and a new highest ideal of desiring that the totality of earthly things eternally return just as they are.

Here at the end I want to recall what I said at the end of my lecture on "Socrates Becomes Socrates." In the *Symposium*, Plato showed Diotima leading Socrates to the insight that is the last stage of his philosophic education, insight into the deep structure of eros as ontology. After this deepest seeing, Plato has Diotima make the long speech on the ladder of loves; what happens at the peak, she says, is both a seeing and a doing. The one who has climbed to the peak *beholds* or sees perfect beauty, and that one *gives birth* or engages in a kind of making or poetizing in the presence of the beautiful. The end of Nietzsche's "History of the I-feeling" gives his first ever completed version of Nietzsche becoming Nietzsche, and his wording is similar to Plato's. There too, it is a matter of beholding and engendering or of seeing and making. The seeing that is a letting the true beings take possession of us leads to the making that is the springing up of "new images of existence" that will rule humanity.

In both Plato and Nietzsche *philosophy* generates *philosophic poetry.*

And here at the very end we come back to Strauss. He said in one of his letters to Klein that when Plato is seen as an exoteric writer, the Plato of "the specifically Platonic philosophy" can be separated from the Plato "nearest my heart." Nearest Strauss's heart is the genuine Plato, the esoteric

Plato who showed Socrates becoming Socrates, gaining his comprehensive understanding of being as becoming, as *eros*. And for me, that is the greatest service Strauss performs for us: he shows us how to read the philosophers and to discover in their exoteric teaching the esoteric understanding it implies, the understanding they intended for those few who resemble them by being driven by the passion to know. For however great Strauss is, and he is great, he is not great in the way Plato and Nietzsche are great: he is not himself a philosopher and philosophic poet as Plato and Nietzsche are. Strauss shows us how to read Plato and Nietzsche together and to understand what they share as philosophers. And it seems to me that Strauss even went beyond that revelation of kinship between these two philosophers: he expressed cautious encouragement of reading Nietzsche as the platonic political philosopher of our time. He gave many indications of this in his late Nietzsche essay; here are three of them.

One: Strauss chose to place this essay out of chronological order at the center of the book he called *Studies in Platonic Political Philosophy*, paired there with "Jerusalem and Athens." With this little device Strauss says: At the center of the study of platonic political philosophy in our time is the study of Jerusalem and Athens and Nietzsche.

Two: Within this essay, Strauss helps us understand just how Nietzsche is a platonic *philosopher*. Strauss says that Nietzsche's conclusion as a philosopher that to be is to be will to power "takes the place which *eros* . . . occupies in Plato's thought." Will to power and eros are ontological doctrines; Nietzsche, like Socrates, has expert knowledge of the erotic things. And Strauss helps us understand how Nietzsche is a platonic *political* philosopher; Nietzsche develops a philosophic poetry that Strauss calls "a relapse into Platonism" because this aspect of Platonism simply belongs to philosophy in its relation to the city/the human community.

Three: As the last sentence of this essay Strauss wrote: *Die vornehme Natur ersetzt die göttliche Natur.* He ended his Nietzsche essay as he ended *The City and Man*, with something he did not want to *pronounce* directly but wanted you to *question* and *wonder about*. For me, that wondering leads to this: "*Noble nature replaces divine nature*" means that nature as Nietzsche teaches it replaces nature as Plato taught it.

Strauss's Nietzsche essay, out of place at the center of his last book, stating that will to power takes the place that eros occupies, with its German last sentence leads me to a conclusion that restates the title of my lectures, "Strauss Plato Nietzsche": Strauss intimates that Nietzsche replaces Plato in our time.

Times change. Gods die. Changed times require of the new philosopher new images of existence. For me, that's the meaning of Nietzsche for our time.

Index

Laurence Lampert (1941–2024) taught for thirty-five years at Indiana University–Purdue University Indianapolis and was the author of eight books of philosophy, most recently *How Socrates Became Socrates* and *What a Philosopher Is: Becoming Nietzsche*. He lived in Winnipeg.